W9-ACG-339

Innovation Systems

World Bank Support of Science and Technology Development

Vinod K. Goel
Ekaterina Koryukin
Mohini Bhatia
Priyanka Agarwal

THE WORLD BANK
Washington, D.C.

World Bank Working Papers are published to communicate the results of the Bank's work to the development community with the least possible delay. The typescript of this paper therefore has not been prepared in accordance with the procedures appropriate to journal printed texts, and the World Bank accepts no responsibility for errors. Some sources cited in this paper may be informal documents that are not readily available.

The findings, interpretations, and conclusions expressed in this paper are entirely those of the author(s) and do not necessarily reflect the views of the Board of Executive Directors of the World Bank or the governments they represent. The World Bank cannot guarantee the accuracy of the data included in this work. The boundaries, colors, denominations, and other information shown on any map in this work do not imply on the part of the World Bank any judgment of the legal status of any territory or the endorsement or acceptance of such boundaries.

The material in this publication is copyrighted. The World Bank encourages dissemination of its work and normally will grant permission for use.

Permission to photocopy items for internal or personal use, for the internal or personal use of specific clients, or for educational classroom use, is granted by the World Bank, provided that the appropriate fee is paid. Please contact the Copyright Clearance Center before photocopying items.
Copyright Clearance Center, Inc.
222 Rosewood Drive
Danvers, MA 01923, U.S.A.
Tel: 978-750-8400 • Fax: 978-750-4470.

For permission to reprint individual articles or chapters, please fax your request with complete information to the Republication Department, Copyright Clearance Center, fax 978-750-4470.

All other queries on rights and licenses should be addressed to the World Bank at the address above, or faxed to 202-522-2422.

ISBN: 0-8213-5837-5
eISBN: 0-8213-5838-3
ISSN: 1726-5878

Vinod K. Goel is a Senior Consultant on Technology Development for the Private and Financial Sector Development Unit of the Europe and Central Asia Region at the World Bank. Ekaterina Koryukin is a Projects Officer at the same unit. Mohini Bhatia is a Consultant. Priyanka Agarwal was a Summer Intern (2003).

Library of Congress Cataloging-in-Publication Data has been requested.

TABLE OF CONTENTS

LIST OF BOXES

LIST OF FIGURES

Acknowledgments

T his paper was prepared by a team comprising Vinod K. Goel, Ekaterina Koryukin and Mohini Bhatia. Priyanka Agarwal and Mohini Bhatia carried out the desk research during Fall 2003. Some of the findings came out of the project preparatory work done for the Croatia—Science and Technology Project. A menu for Knowledge Economy operations, included as Annex A, was developed by the team to streamline the design of Knowledge Economy projects in the Europe and Central Asia Region. The project database (Annex B) was compiled using data in Image Bank.

Special thanks are given to Anil Sood (Vice President, SFRVP, and Acting Director, ECSPF), and Sector Managers (ECSPF) who supported the team in the preparation and completion of this paper. The team is grateful to Dr. R. A. Mashelkar (Council of Scientific and Industrial Research, India), Dr. Sanjaya Lall (Oxford University, UK), Melvin Goldman (Cornell University, former Bank staff) and Lauritz Holm-Nielsen (Lead Education Specialist, the World Bank) who were peer reviewers for this paper.

ABBREVIATIONS

CSIR	Council for Scientific and Industrial Research, India
ECU	European Customs Union
EU	European Union
FDI	Foreign Direct Investment
HR	Human Resources
ICT	Information and Communication Technologies
IFC	International Finance Corporation
IPR	Intellectual Property Rights
ISO	International Standards Organization
IT	Information Technology
ITP	Industrial Technology Project
KE	Knowledge-based Economy
M&E	Monitoring and Evaluation
MAM	Marmara Research Center (Turkey)
MIS	Management Information Systems
MSI	Millennium Science Initiative
MSTQ	Metrology, Standards, Testing, and Quality
NGO	Non-governmental Organization
PAL	Programmatic Adjustment Loan
R&D	Research and Development
RDI	Research and Development Institution
S&T	Science and Technology
SMEs	Small and Medium-Size Enterprises
STP	Science and Technology Project
TDF	Technology Development Financing
TI	Technology Institution
TSS	Technology Support Services
TTGV	Technology Development Foundation of Turkey
UME	National Metrology Institute (Turkey)
VC	Venture Capital
VCC	Venture Capital Company
VCF	Venture Capital Fund
WTO	World Trade Organization

EXECUTIVE SUMMARY

T he capacity of a society to produce, select, adapt, and commercialize knowledge is critical for trade, competitiveness, and for the sustained growth of the economy. The World Bank's *World Development Report 1999* states:

> Today's most technologically advanced economies are truly knowledge-based, . . . creating millions of knowledge-related jobs in an array of disciplines that have emerged overnight. . . . the need for developing countries to increase their capacity to use knowledge cannot be overstated.

Enhancing this capacity is becoming a prerequisite for improving productivity and increasing the welfare of society. The knowledge economy (KE) can be defined through analysis of four characteristic areas (the "four pillars" of the knowledge economy): (a) the policy and institutional framework; (b) an innovation system; (c) education and lifelong learning; and (d) information technology infrastructure and electronic development ("e-development").

The World Bank experience in promoting knowledge-based economies is dominated by projects focused on innovation systems support including science industrial technology development. The education and e-development aspects in relation to a knowledge-based economy are less explored. Through its knowledge economy policy and institutional framework the Bank has supported many KE programs, both in the form of investment projects that have made provisions for specific components and through adjustment operations that have included reforms of a general nature, the latter typically to enhance competitiveness, to ease information exchange, or to provide economic incentives for private sector participation in technology ventures.

This paper concentrates on innovation systems support projects financed by the Bank during 1990–2003, together with a few successful earlier examples. It reviews some 51 projects involving over US$4.2 billion in Bank support, with individual projects ranging from US$3 million to US$300 million, mean project size has been about US$58 million.

The Bank has gained significant experience and has an important role to play in supporting innovation systems projects. Examples of successful programs include those undertaken in the Republic of Korea, India, Indonesia, Turkey, Brazil, and Chile. The Bank's role typically has been to facilitate and augment reform efforts through its experiences around the world and play the role of an "honest broker" between the productive and S&T sectors in institutional reforms. On the institution-building side, the Bank contributes in its capacity as a facilitator of the reform process in bringing together relevant partners for each of the institutions that would advise and participate in building institutional capabilities. This enhances the effectiveness of the design and delivery of services and the sustainability of these activities for the future. The Bank's involvement also encourages that difficult measures are taken; including, for example, the raising of institutional accountability. Prudent market tests are applied to the various available interventions and fiscal discipline is imposed on institutions that are in the process of restructuring. Drawing on its experience in other countries the Bank can provide the long-term support, advice, and leverage needed during the restructuring phase for institutions that seek to attain greater fiscal independence and that seek to enhance the quality of their services and their contribution to the national economy.

Innovation Systems Support

The ultimate objective of a well-functioning innovation system is to serve the needs of the economy by achieving better integration of the science and technology (S&T) infrastructure with production needs, by increasing private sector participation in technology development, and by developing stronger linkages between industry, universities, and research institutions. Innovation system projects normally focus on building:

- an environment conducive to business development (putting in place, for example, key national policies, an intellectual property rights (IPR) regime, an appropriate quality and standards system, and a metrology system);
- a framework for the generation of new ideas (through tax incentives, IPR protection, and competitive research programs), support in determining the feasibility of research outputs and their subsequent commercialization (technology financing programs, IPR support), and support for the establishment of new businesses (venture capital, start-up funds); and
- enterprise-level support to establish new KE-based companies, to carry out research and development (R&D) activities, and to generate and sustain revenues (incubators, technology centers, technoparks).

Measurements, standards, testing, and quality systems (MSTQ). A weak MSTQ system can impede industry's ability to compete effectively. Upgrading the framework for MSTQ thus often is a necessary first step in improving the innovation system (as well as being essential for World Trade Organization compliance and accession to the European Union). Many traditional S&T projects contain some components of MSTQ support; for example, setting up or upgrading institutes dealing with MSTQ, such as metrology organizations, standards institutions, and quality and accreditation councils. Bank projects also pay special attention to separating the private and public aspects of MSTQ by privatizing (or setting up as private) income-generating entities such as testing laboratories and certification bodies and by centralizing functions of a public-good nature, such as national metrology institutes and national standards offices (and thus minimizing the conflicts of interest that arise where regulations are developed by the same entities that provide accreditation and certification). For example, the Turkey Industrial Technology Project upgraded the National Metrology Institute that will serve more than 80 percent of Turkish industry metrology needs, and the Indonesia Industrial Technology Development Project upgraded the National Metrology Center to provide better services to small and medium-size enterprises.

Intellectual property rights (IPR) regime. An effective IPR regime is essential for commercializing research outputs and for technology transfer, especially after other reforms in S&T take hold, as well as for enhancing the competitiveness of industry. Many Bank projects have included IPR support in one form or another, from setting up or upgrading national-level patent offices to setting up individual

IPR units in universities or research and development institutions. Other projects have supported the needs of research communities at the micro level or have trained patent agents, judges, and industry personnel. The Mexico Science and Technology Infrastructure Project, for example, supported the creation of the Mexican Institute of Industrial Property, significantly reducing delays in the award of patents, increasing enforcement activities, and increasing the frequency of inspections related to intellectual property violations. Chile's Science for the Knowledge Economy Project also aims to strengthen intellectual property rights regime, with an emphasis on patents. Similarly, the Turkey Industrial Technology Project has strengthened the Turkish Patent Institute to improve the IPR services.

Research and Development Institutions (RDIs). The R&D sector in most developing countries typically comprises a number of public institutions and a good academic base. These tend to be public- and inward-focused, however, and largely disconnected from the needs of industry. Most Bank S&T projects thus aim to strengthen and reorient public research and development institutes to serve the economy while preserving their public good nature. The objective of such effort is ultimately to make a shift in thinking so that Research *and* Development transforms into Research *for* Development, where "*R*" becomes socially meaningful when it leads to "*D*" and when output is inducted into socioeconomic system. Many projects have supported building a framework and appropriate incentives to encourage cooperation between the research community and industry, by, for example, enhancing the incentives for applied research, improving the marketing and commercialization functions of RDIs, introducing competitive research programs, promoting joint projects with industry, universities, and other R&D organizations, and introducing a strategic approach to the commercialization of R&D outputs. Traditional support to RDIs includes the upgrading of physical infrastructure, the improvement of management information systems, and the modernization of management and human resources functions and other business processes. Successful examples include the several national R&D laboratories of the Council for Scientific and Industrial Research (CSIR) in India and the network of R&D institutes at the Marmara Research Center (MAM) in Turkey. Restructuring of both of these institutions increased the share of their contractual research that serves industry and consequently greater usage and adaptation of the R&D by the industry, and many other positive spill-over effects for the economies of these countries. CSIR doubled its income from applied research and MAM increased the proportion of its research that supports industry to around 49 percent in 2003. Building up on the project accomplishments, India was able to attract large research contracts from outside of the country (for example, the largest General Electric's R&D center outside of the United States is located in India and employs about 2,000 people). Increase in applied research in India also gave boost to the development of the biotechnology sector resulting in India now holding a prominent place worldwide (the United States leading) in the biotechnology development area.

Upgrading innovation capabilities of enterprises. In addition to providing the infrastructure that enables the development of new ideas, it is important to provide a framework that also encourages the establishment and nurturing of the knowledge-based companies that can bring these new ideas to commercialization. In this regard, Bank projects have: (a) helped finance the development of new ideas through technology financing institutions, technology financing programs, including the venture capital; (b) set up and helped develop knowledge-based companies through incubator programs and technology and R&D centers; and (c) helped existing companies to upgrade their capabilities and the quality of their services and products through the acquisition and adaptation of new technologies, by funding matching loan/grant schemes and outreach programs.

Bank support for firm-level technology development typically has focused on technology financing institutions and programs. Financing provided through such projects is typically low-interest, and in some cases is made in the form of grants. The financial instruments employed by Bank-supported technology financing entities include loans (no-interest, low-interest, commercial interest, and conditional), grants (usually matching grants), equity participation (sometimes through venture capital programs), royalties, and guarantees. Examples of technology financing programs included the Technology Development Financing program, the Technology Support Services program, and Venture Capital schemes supported by the Industrial Technology Project in Turkey; R&D Programs and venture capital schemes supported by the Industrial Technology Development Project in India, and earlier programs in the Republic of Korea.

Monitoring and evaluation (M&E). Public support for technology sector is justified in large part by its public-good nature. As a consequence it is difficult to measure its value in the conventional terms of net present value or financial rate of return. That said, it is imperative that investments in this area be monitored for their ability to achieve the desired impact. The approach in many cases has been to carry out empirical analysis of benefits to the economy (growth of new businesses and exports, market share held by R&D companies, growth in R&D expenditure and foreign direct investment, and other indicators measuring spill-over effects); and to monitor project-specific performance indicators such as number of patents, number of joint with the industry projects, self-sufficiency ratios, and percent of R&D projects commercialized.

Lessons. Technology projects normally include a spectrum of interventions that are complementary and holistic in nature. On the supply side, the projects reorient public research and development institutes toward industry, build up a functioning measurements, testing, standards and quality system to improve product competitiveness, and protect industry with an effective intellectual property rights regime. On the demand side, they support the use by industry of new technology, through technoparks, technology centers, and incubators, and provide financial support, through technology financing programs, venture capital, and start-up funds, for example. Technology projects as a result typically are complex, contain multiple components of complementary character, and must be run over the long term, frequently within a series of projects. The composition of S&T projects is unique for each country and may combine elements from any of these areas.

Given the nature of technology development, and the newness in many countries of development activities, project design must include an appropriate degree of flexibility. For example, unallocated funds could be reassigned to priority activities that are performing well, pilot initiatives should be considered to determine the viability of different project components, and annual business plans should be periodically reviewed and updated.

Private sector participation is important in the restructuring process for its ability to improve efficiency, management capability, and governance; to embrace stakeholder participation; and to deliver cost effectiveness in overall design and delivery. Bank programs also have welcomed cofinancing from the private sector and have found advisory boards with private sector representation to be particularly valuable in maintaining the business focus, such that delivers the maximum benefit for the economy.

Finally, projects targeting the restructuring of the technology sector are typically labor- and resource-intensive and require strong championship within the government and institutions. This is true for all Bank projects, but especially so for technology related ones given the difficult nature of the reforms and possible resistance within the R&D community, as well as the fact that innovation agenda may be put off the priority lists of busy governments struggling with budget deficits and other macro-economic difficulties. This also makes intensive supervision by experienced Bank staff, continuity and flexibility even more important if the projects are to achieve a lasting change in the mindset of the host country institutions.

CHAPTER I

INTRODUCTION

Innovation systems and science and technology (S&T) projects supported by the World Bank have taken on many forms in the past several years. The Bank's involvement in industrial technology projects started in the 1970s, with Israel and Spain numbering among the first countries to receive support in the form of industrial technology development.[1] This paper reviews the lessons learned in S&T projects that have been supported by the Bank, with an emphasis on the examples of the past decade (1989–2003). Projects and their components were included in this review if their objectives included the use of scientific and technological knowledge to improve development. The review included 51 project, in an aggregate amount of over US$4.2 billion; this did not include agricultural research projects where the Bank supported a significant amount of projects world-wide. The amounts invested in individual projects ranged from US$3 million to US$300 million, with a mean project size of about US$58 million.

This paper first discusses the concept of the knowledge-based economy (KE) and its relation with the S&T sector, and then identifies the main themes of KE projects, groups them by the four pillars of the knowledge economy, and summarizes the key lessons learned. Since the Bank experience is most substantial in the areas of innovation systems and related policy frameworks, this review focuses on industrial technology development and on building national innovation systems. It touches only briefly on the themes of education, and information and communications technology, with the aim only of providing the proper context for the main study. A List of Projects is included in Box 1, and brief descriptions of these projects in Annex B to this report.

---

1. The term "R&D" describes "Applied R&D" and the terms "R&D" and "Technology Development" are used interchangeably throughout this paper.

CHAPTER 2

BACKGROUND

*T*he knowledge economy. The capacity of a society to produce, select, adapt, and commercialize knowledge is critical for trade, competitiveness, sustained economic growth, and quality of life. The World Bank's *World Development Report 1999* states that:

> Today's most technologically advanced economies are truly knowledge-based, . . . creating millions of knowledge-related jobs in an array of disciplines that have emerged overnight. . . . [T]he need for developing countries to increase their capacity to use knowledge cannot be overstated.

Enhancing this capacity is becoming a prerequisite for improving productivity and the welfare of society. The Organization for Economic Cooperation and Development (OECD) similarly has concluded that the "underlying long-term growth rates in OECD economies depend on maintaining and expanding the knowledge base."

As the last few decades have shown, two strong simultaneous shifts in the global economy have led to knowledge becoming a key factor of production. First, the Internet revolution has greatly reduced the cost and increased the capacity of firms and organizations to store, process, manipulate, and distribute information. Second, globalization has opened domestic industry to international competition, making the ability to compete in global markets vital for long-term success. As information becomes more accessible and less expensive, and as globalization becomes an integrated part of competition, the skills and competencies relating to the selection and efficient use of knowledge are becoming more critical.

A handful of the world's richest countries produce the overwhelming majority of new scientific and technological knowledge, and it is these countries that derive the greatest benefit from its use (OECD 2003; see Figure 1). Most of the rest of the world's nations are struggling, with varying degrees of success, to establish scientific and technological research systems able to invigorate their economies and provide solutions to their social needs. Unfortunately for developing countries, globalization and the information revolution favor the scientifically strong. Countries that want to improve their knowledge base face a huge task to close the gap that separates them from scientifically advanced countries.

BOX 1: BANK: SCIENCE AND TECHNOLOGY PROJECTS (1989–2003)

Fiscal Year	Region	Country	Project	Loan Amt. US$ million
under prep	ECA	Croatia	Science and Technology Project	38.0
under prep	ECA	Turkey	Knowledge and Innovation Project	100.0
under prep	ECA	Russia	Technology Commercialization Project	50.0
under prep	ECA	Romania	Knowledge Economy Project	50.0
2003	ECA	Ukraine	eDevelopment Project	5.0
2003	LAC	Honduras	Trade Facilitation and Productivity Enhancement Project	25.0
2003	LAC	Chile	Science for the Knowledge Economy Project	25.0
2003	AFR	Congo	Private Sector Development and Competitiveness Project	12.0
2003	SAR	India	Technical Engineering Education Quality Improvement Project	250.0
2002	MNA	Yemen	Higher Education Project	5.0
2002	EAP	Indonesia	Global Distance Learning Network Project	2.6
2002	MNA	Egypt	Higher Education Enhancement Project	50.0
2002	ECA	Armenia	Enterprise Incubator Project	5.0
2001	LAC	Nicaragua	Competitiveness Project	50.0
2001	LAC	Venezuela	Millennium Science Initiative	5.0
2000	LAC	Chile	Millennium Science Initiative	5.0
2000	ECA	Turkey	Industrial Technology Project	155.0
2000	EAP	China	Higher Education Reform Project	50.0
1999	LAC	Chile	Higher Education Improvement Project	145.5
1999	LAC	Mexico	Knowledge and Innovation Project	300.0
1998	LAC	Brazil	Science and Technology Reform Support Project	155.0
1998	EAP	Indonesia	Information Infrastructure Development Project	34.5
1997	EAP	Thailand	Secondary Education Quality Improvement Project	194.7
1996	ECA	Russia	Standards Development Project	24.0
1996	EAP	Thailand	Universities Science and Engineering Education Project	143.4
1996	EAP	Indonesia	Industrial Technology Development Project	38.5
1996	EAP	China	Technology Development Project	200.0
1996	AFR	Mauritius	Higher and Technical Education Project	16.0
1995	AFR	Ghana	Private Sector Development Project	13.0
1995	LAC	Brazil	Science and Technology Subprogram: Science Centers and Directed Research	15.8
1995	EAP	Indonesia	Second Professional Human Resource Development Project	69.0
1995	EAP	Indonesia	University Research for Graduate Education Project	58.9
1995	AFR	Mauritius	Competitiveness Enhancement Project	6.7
1994	EAP	Korea	Science and Technical Education Project	190.0
1994	EAP	Malaysia	Polytechnic Development Project	107.0
1993	MNA	Tunisia	Higher Education Restructuring Project	75.0
1993	LAC	Mexico	Science and Technology Infrastructure	189.0
1993	EAP	Korea	Science Education and Libraries Computerization Project	50.0
1992	EAP	Philippines	Engineering and Science Education Project	85.0

(continued)

Box 1: Bank: Science and Technology Projects (1989–2003) (Continued)

Fiscal Year	Region	Country	Project	Loan Amt. US$ million
1992	ECA	Turkey	Technology Development Project	100.0
1992	AFR	Kenya	Universities Investment Project	55.0
1991	MNA	Algeria	Science and Technology University Development Project	65.0
1991	EAP	China	Rural Industrial Technology (SPARK) Project	95.1
1991	ECA	Hungary	Human Resources Development Project	150.0
1991	LAC	Brazil	Science and Research Development Project	150.0
1991	EAP	Korea	Third Technology Advancement Project	60.0
1990	EAP	Korea	Universities Science and Technology Project	45.0
1990	SAR	India	Industrial Technology Project	200.0
1989	ECA	Hungary	Third Industrial Restructuring Project	140.0
1985	EAP	Korea	Second Technology Development Project	50.0
1982	EAP	Korea	First Technology Development Project	50.0
1979	EAP	Korea	Korea Electronics Technology Project	29.0
			Total Funding	4,253

The term "Knowledge Economy" is used to describe the new economic environment in which innovation and knowledge are replacing capital and labor as the primary wealth-creating assets. The creation and use of knowledge is not necessarily focused only on the high-technology industries, however—all industries need to use technology to maintain their competitiveness. Even in the more traditional agricultural and manufacturing sectors, knowledge (about crop varieties, new markets, or innovative production processes) is becoming more easily and rapidly accessible on a global basis, and its competitive value thus is increasing. For the more sophisticated economies, the next step in enhancing their competitiveness lies in creating an environment conducive to the transition of concepts and new ideas to real products. This requires a reorientation toward market industry and a well-functioning national innovation system, together with the integration of research and development institutions, universities and academia, and the private business sector.

An example of a region-wide initiative to become a knowledge-based society is the European Union's Lisbon Strategy.[2] Three priorities that have been identified by the Lisbon Strategy in this area include improving investment in networks and knowledge, strengthening competitiveness in industry and services, and promoting life-long learning. Following the strategy, while a lot more work would need to be done to achieve the goals, the EU countries have achieved some progress: 6 million jobs created since 1999, in spite of the economic slowdown; significant improvements in long-term unemployment and the rate of female employment; opening up to competition of several strategic network markets (such as telecommunications, energy, and rail freight); internet take-up in schools, businesses, public administrations and households.

The primary focus for all countries at all stages of development toward a knowledge-based economy must be to build on their competitive advantage. For example, in the late 1980s Finland's economy was predominantly based on the forest industry (76 percent of Finland is forest) and was as a consequence vulnerable to the cyclical nature of the raw materials. Exports accounted for about 5 percent of GDP. Through large investment in R&D and a policy of innovation, Fin-

---

2. The Lisbon Strategy is a commitment to bring about economic, social and environmental renewal in the European Union. In March 2000, the European Council in Lisbon set out a ten-year strategy to make the EU the world's most dynamic and competitive economy.

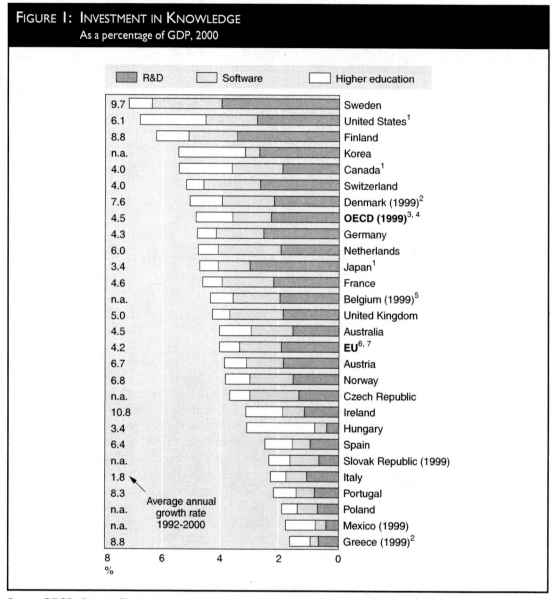

FIGURE 1: INVESTMENT IN KNOWLEDGE
As a percentage of GDP, 2000

Source: OECD, Science, Technology and Industry Scorecard 2003. Copyright OECD 2003.
http://www1.oecd.org/publications/e-book/92-2003-04-1-7294/pdf/A1.pdf

land has expanded and diversified its exports to include the supply of wood and paper products and machinery, and exports now make up 20 percent of GDP. The country furthermore has captured a 20 percent global market share in the wood and paper industry (Finnish Forest Industries Federation 2003). Finland's achievements were particularly unique due to the simultaneous expansion in the high-technology industry as well, with Nokia. Finland has surpassed the US, according to latest OECD indicators (2003) in certain sectors such as size and growth of the information and communications technologies (ICT) sector, price of Internet access, high-skilled ICT workers for the information economy, scientific publications, and even in number of researchers per total employment (OECD 2003).

The challenge of achieving a turnaround as dramatic as Finland's may be very difficult for smaller countries than larger ones. In larger countries, the focus should be on regional development; for example, parts of India are among the poorest in the world, but the country also has a dynamic and fast-growing information technology software and service industry. This largely became possible due to the promotion of excellent education as well as willingness of the Government of India to permit in mid-1990s liberalized captive satellite communications by companies exporting IT services and products. The National Association of Software and Service Companies today estimates that Indian software and services sector will post a 28 percent growth in 2003–04 at $12 billion in revenues, compared to $9.5 billion in 2002–03. The sector's annual exports are worth around US$8 billion in 2003, accounting for 16 percent of all exports, and are growing rapidly and are expected to reach US$50 billion this decade. Larger developing countries must identify and build on pockets of development such as this where the country may have a comparative advantage: industrial base, cultural background and human resource base, entrepreneurial skills, or economic and political systems.

Building Innovations Systems: The World Bank experience. The Bank has significant experience in technology projects, through successful programs in countries including India (Box 4), the Republic of Korea (Box 5), Turkey (Box 6), Spain, Israel, Indonesia, Brazil, China (Box 7), Chile (Box 8), and Mexico (Box 9), and has an important role to play in supporting future projects. Annex A, a Menu of Operations, includes a list of possible activities that have been and may be supported in the future by the Bank projects; composition of each project would be unique depending on the country needs. The Bank's engagement in industrial technology projects began in the 1970s with a component in Israel's Industrial Development Loan, approved in 1975, to improve product design and production processes to reorient industry toward exports. The Bank's first complete project for industrial technology was in Spain, this time aimed to improve the import and use of technologies to raise competitiveness and increase exports. A series of projects followed. The Korea Electronics Technology Project, approved in 1979, aimed to reorient the Republic of Korea's R&D sector toward the semiconductor industry and led to a series of industrial technology development and technical training projects; and in the 1980s projects were initiated in China and Indonesia to build R&D capacity through an emphasis on higher education and technical training. The initial projects in Spain and Korea were implemented by public institutions; one of obstacles faced in these projects resulted from not having private sector financing handled by independent bodies with professional management and banking capabilities. Heeding this lesson, in the 1980s the Bank changed the way that it supported these types of projects. Bank involvement instead aimed to help catalyze private sector participation in technology development, shifting the emphasis away from a public-sector-driven and less efficient approach to one driven by the needs of industry and the economy. Currently, the Bank is engaged in preparation of the second-generation projects targeted at building knowledge-based economies in Croatia, Turkey, Bulgaria, Romania, and other countries. These projects, in addition to more traditional policy reforms and innovation support activities, include support for e-Development, e-Government and other aspects to improve information flows and transparency.

The Bank's role typically has been to accelerate and augment reform efforts through its experiences around the world and play the role of an "honest broker" between the public productive and S&T sectors in institutional reforms. On the institution-building side, the Bank contributes in its capacity as a facilitator of the reform process in bringing together relevant partners for each of the institutions that would advise and participate in building institutional capabilities. This enhances the effectiveness of the design and delivery of services and the sustainability of these activities for the future. The Bank's involvement also encourages that difficult measures are taken; including, for example, the raising of institutional accountability. Prudent market tests are applied to the various available interventions and fiscal discipline is imposed on institutions that are in the process of restructuring. Drawing on its experience in other countries the Bank can provide the long-term support, advice, and leverage needed during the restructuring phase for institutions that seek to attain greater fiscal independence and that seek to enhance the quality of their services and their contribution to the national economy.

The underlying themes of efforts to improve the innovation capacity of an economy have been the introduction of market competition, the development of exports, efforts to attract foreign direct investment, and efforts to promote and protect local ideas and inventions. The work done in these areas has included the upgrading of technological capability at the enterprise level, to incorporate foreign technologies and processes; standardization of processes; skills upgrading of the workforce; and the building of local entrepreneurial capabilities. This has required a shift in the incentive framework for applied research, the development of linkages between R&D community and industry, the financing of innovation, and a shift from a supply-side-driven R&D approach to a demand-driven one. In most countries where S&T projects of this nature have been launched, liberalization reforms also have been underway, in turn also raising expectations for an increase in demand for R&D services and products.

Bank assistance in the knowledge-based economy arena has included not only assistance in developing the private and financial sectors, but also significant work in the agriculture sector and education. In a number of countries the Bank also has supported the development of information and communications technologies (ICT) infrastructure. The Bank's most diverse and substantial experience has come in the innovation, science and technology development, however, where it has supported the upgrading of intellectual property rights regimes, the improvement of measurements, standards, testing, and quality systems, and the restructuring of research and development institutions and has provided assistance to enterprises to develop, adapt, use, and commercialize new technologies. The Bank has also supported the setting up of technoparks and venture capital funds. The support of innovation development is effective and more sustainable if it is accompanied by appropriate adjustments in the policy framework and by the introduction of economic incentives, as well as by coordinated efforts to reorient education and training toward industry needs. A good ICT backbone is also crucial if such interventions are to fully realize their potential.

There is a wide number of proponents of knowledge economy projects in the Bank and a lot of support has been provided to the teams working in this area in the recent years including setting the arena for cross sector collaboration between the regions, sectors and networks across the Bank, the bulk of analytical research carried out to-date, and such regional initiatives as analytical framework set by the Regional Chief Economist's (for the Latin America and Caribbean Region) recent Flagship Reports (De Ferranti et al. 2003). While the stages and main focus of innovation support projects vary across the World they all follow the same goal of setting the framework and incentives to stimulate industry upgrading through use of better technologies, allow wider access to pertinent information for citizens in order to contribute to making more efficient use of public resources, and, ultimately, to economic growth.

The text boxes interspersed throughout this paper further describe activities and projects from a country-based view, outlining how different countries have created institutions, implemented major reforms, and strengthened their innovation capacity through partnerships with the World Bank.

CHAPTER 3

THE FOUR PILLARS OF THE KNOWLEDGE ECONOMY

The growth of a global knowledge-based economy creates great opportunities and poses interesting challenges for all countries, but particularly for those that are struggling to combat widespread poverty and to promote sustainable development, those with weak political, administrative, and economic institutions, and those dealing with the difficult transition from a centralized to a market economy. To take advantage of the opportunities and navigate these risks, a country must undergo major reform. First, it must develop a coherent, multifaceted national strategy for building and sustaining a knowledge-based economy. Key to this strategy is development of a mindset that is open to change and knowledge sharing. Second, it must provide the environment, including infrastructure for the networking and sharing of knowledge, to ensure cooperation and coordination between and the balanced development of key sectors of the economy. Third, it must develop and implement this strategy in a participatory, broad-based fashion that includes and empowers all major sectors of society, including the private sector, educators, scientists and innovators, civil society, the media, and others. These strategic reforms may be classified under the "four pillars" of the knowledge economy (Dahlman 1999; see Box 2).

The full integration of the four pillars of the knowledge economy is the key means by which a country can enhance its competitiveness in international markets and propel its economy toward its maximum social, political, and economic potential. The focus of this paper is to elaborate on Innovation systems development pillar and related policy frameworks, while touching only briefly on the themes of education and information and communication technology.

Policy and Institutional Framework

Reforms always need a solid support on the policy level to take root. The support of a country's economic development would ultimately include policy reforms to promote competition, ease of exit and entry of firms, deepen financial sector, reform enterprise sector, modernize tax system, promote foreign direct investment, rule of law, open trade, flexible labor market, etc. The policy framework of a knowledge-based society in its turn would focus on elements that allow free information flows among the governments, businesses and citizens, provide incentive for private sector participation in different sectors, stimulate public and private sector collaboration to serve the needs of the economy,

---

BOX 2: THE FOUR PILLARS OF A KNOWLEDGE ECONOMY

Policy and Institutional Framework. Creating an appropriate economic incentive and institutional regime that encourages the widespread and efficient use of local and global knowledge in all sectors of the economy, that fosters entrepreneurship, and that permits and supports the economic and social transformations engendered by the knowledge revolution.

Innovation System. Creating an efficient innovation system and business environment that encourages innovation and entrepreneurship, comprising firms, science and research centers, universities, think tanks, and other organizations that can tap into and contribute to the growing stock of global knowledge, that can adapt it to local needs, and that can use it to create new products, services, and ways of doing business.

Education and Training. Creating a society of skilled, flexible, and creative people, with opportunities for a good education and life-long learning available to all, and a flexible and appropriate mix of public and private funding.

Information Infrastructure (ICT/e-Development). Building a dynamic information infrastructure and a competitive and innovative information sector that fosters a variety of efficient and competitive ICT services and tools, available for all sectors of society. This includes not only high-end technologies such as the Internet and mobile telephony, but also radio, television, and other media; computers and other devices for storing, processing, and using information; and a range of communication services.

---

and promote business opportunities, investments and growth. The Innovation System reform then would step in to build and modernize intellectual property rights regime and measurement, testing, standards, and quality systems, restructure research and development institutions, provide incentives to the industry and small and medium enterprises to use, adapt and develop new technologies, as well as stimulate development of various mechanisms to finance the technology (Box 3). While broad policy reforms such as business environment could be an agenda on its own, the knowledge-economy, and innovation systems policy reforms in particular, are better supported as components and conditionality of investment projects and reinforced within larger adjustment and programmatic operations.

Innovation Systems

Knowledge is transformed into goods and services through a country's national innovation system. Its benefits become evident when it is employed within a complementary system of: (a) knowledge-producing organizations in the education and training system, such as universities and research institutes; (b) macroeconomic and regulatory framework, including trade policies that affect technology diffusion; (c) communications infrastructure; and (d) diverse other factors, such as access to the global knowledge base. The ultimate objective of a well-functioning innovation system is to serve the needs of the economy by achieving full integration of S&T infrastructure with the production base, by increasing private sector participation in innovation and technology development, and by developing strong linkages between industry, universities, and research institutions.

National innovation systems are effective only to the extent that the different elements work in harmony, however. A multi-pronged structure must be built to support national innovation from the birth of an idea to its ultimate commercialization and production. The environment must be conducive to entrepreneurship, with key national policies, intellectual property rights protection, and an appropriate system of standards and quality in place. There must be a functioning framework for the generation of new ideas by research institutions, universities, and private firms, as well as for the industry using these research products. Financing must be available for the enterprises to use, adapt, and develop new technologies, as well as there must be a framework to support the establishment, and sustainability of knowledge-based firms.

There is a tendency among most countries to concentrate on adjusting input parameters, such as the number of researchers. While such structural enhancements may be necessary they are not

Box 3: Main Policy Reforms to Support Innovations Agenda

Intellectual Property Rights and Measurement, Testing, Standards and Quality:
- Provide laws and regulations to be compatible with international and regional practices.

Research and Development Institutions (RDIs):
- Create conducive environment for public RDIs and their staff to engage in contractual research and commercialization of R&D;
- Provide RDIs with appropriate flexibility and autonomy in managing their activities, including budget allocation and human resources (including hiring and promotion of scientists);
- Introduce incentives for applied research and financial sustainability;
- Consolidate R&D system to be more efficient and less burdensome on the public budget;
- Reform relevant laws to enhance the framework for R&D and innovation:
  - decentralizing the management and financing of higher education institutions and programs, reducing university and research institute fragmentation, and developing quality control for these institutions and programs

Incentives for Industry (especially SMEs) to develop, adapt and commercialize new technologies:
- Promote growth of knowledge-based companies and commercialization of research outputs;
- R&D tax incentives, upgrade labor skills, reform of public procurement, technology parks, incubators.

Financing Instruments to support technology development:
- Provide appropriate legal and regulatory framework and business environment for potential investors;
- Create technology financing institutions, R&D financing instruments—such as loans, equity, venture capital, and start-up funds, etc.

Box 4: India

Industrial Technology Development Project
Project approved: December 1989. Project completed: June 1998. Loan: US$200 million

The objective of this project was to facilitate the acquisition and development of technology by industrial firms in India. It aimed to balance existing domestic technological capability with the import of foreign technology, and to reduce the financial constraints on new technology ventures and the foreign exchange constraint on technology imports. The project helped small, innovative firms obtain financing by supporting the development of venture capital in India, in the form of six VC companies managing nine VC funds. These VC companies invested in more than 300 firms, producing returns that have averaged 18–20 percent. The project in essence launched the VC industry in India, but its indirect contribution—introducing a culture of risk finance and thus attracting foreign venture capitalists to India—may have been equally important. The project additionally supported the upgrading of RDIs, providing technology services to industry and promoting collaboration between industry and research institutions. The project provided loans rather than grants, forcing the borrower institutions to focus on their financial management and rates of return. A number of research institutes were able to modernize and upgrade their physical facilities, enabling them to enter new areas of research and to reorient themselves to serve industry. Finally, the project also financed the importation of technology and technical know-how by supporting the fast-track Technology Development Fund, which put forward US$100 million to benefit 600–800 firms.

Technical Education Engineering Quality Improvement Project
Project approved: 2003. Loan: US$250 million

This project aims to improve the quality of engineering institutions throughout India. The country has six Indian Institutes of Technology (IITs) that every year send large percent of their graduates to work for foreign multinationals, both in India or abroad. Initially the project proposed increasing the number of IITs in India, but based on Mashelkar Committee report it was determined that upgrading existing regional engineering and technical institutions would be more resource-efficient and would produce a wider supply of qualified specialists to better meet the needs of industry. The institutions are being selected based on their willingness to accept academic, financial, managerial, and administrative autonomy, increase cost-recovery ratios, etc. The number of institutions to be selected is expected to be 20–25.

sufficient for the successful creation of an innovating economy. A shift in thinking toward output parameters, such as the share of exports held by high-value-added products, is required. Bank inter-ventions in the building of innovation systems have been comprehensive. They have included the upgrading of measurements, standards, testing and quality systems; the creation of institutional infrastructure for quality enhancement and certification; alignment of technology regulations with World Trade Organization standards and regional requirements, such as the European Customs Union standards; strengthening of intellectual property rights regimes; restructuring of public research and development institutions; supporting technology financing programs and technical assistance grants; establishment of venture capital funds; and support of firm-level innovation and technology development, including establishment of technology centers and technoparks. Much of this has been achieved with significant private sector participation.

Project outcomes have varied with the country context and development objectives. The innovation system has been successful in several cases where it has used institutional linkages, international participation, and a systemic approach to move ideas from concept to product. In other cases the reform process has set broader objectives requiring technology institutions and scientists to respond to changed incentives, such as reorienting research toward applications and industry needs, increasing the amount of contractual research, and building international linkages and other goals. In such cases the momentum and commitment have needed to be mainstreamed for wide acceptance. For example, the Republic of Korea's Technology Development Project has advanced to a third stage in a series that was initiated in the early 1980s when the Bank and the government set up the Korea Technology Development Corporation (KTDC). In its first 10 years of operation KTDC assisted nearly 3,000 projects in their technology needs. The approved funding amounted to about US$830 million (both from the Government and the Bank), 73 percent of which went to in-house research activities, 2 percent to technology imports, 23 percent to commercialization, and 2 percent to the purchase of research equipment.

Measurements, Standards, Testing and Quality (MSTQ) system. A weak MSTQ system can impede industry's ability to compete. The demand for reliable MSTQ services is expected to increase in the future, despite an evident lack of awareness among companies of the potential benefits of quality certification and standardization. Upgrading the framework for MSTQ is a basic requirement and a first step in improving the innovation system—as it helps level the playing field, in international terms. A strong MSTQ system furthermore is necessary for World Trade Organization compliance and other regional requirements, such as accession to the European Union, for example. Many S&T projects contain a component of such a system, through the setting up or upgrading of institutions: the first Technology Development Project in Turkey resulted in the setting up of the National Metrology Institute (UME) that on com-pletion of the project (in 1998) was capable of meeting roughly 30–40 percent of Turkish industry's metrology needs. The follow-up Industrial Technology Project, which continued the upgrade of UME, has enabled it to meet 80 percent of metrology needs in the country by early 2004 (expected to grow to 96 percent by 2006). The project provided investments into both upgrade of Turkey's metrology physical infrastructure (building new laboratories and purchasing up-to-date equipment) but also modernizing its management structure and busi-ness processes and marketing capabilities. The setting up of this metrology center has greatly enhanced measurement capabilities in Turkey, lowering the costs of metrology to firms and making measurement facilities available locally to smaller firms that would not otherwise have used them. The Turkish Standards Institute additionally was strengthened through the setting up of the Quality Campus in Istanbul and staff training and technical assistance. The expansion and upgrading of the country's standards infrastructure has helped industrial competitiveness by improving quality standards and providing internationally acceptable certification to Turkish exporters. Similarly, Indonesia's Industrial Technology Development Project upgraded the National Metrology Center to provide better service to small and medium enterprises. Russia's

Standards Development Project, Brazil's Science and Technology Reform Support Project, and China's Technology Development Project also included components for the upgrading of metrology and standards institutes and services.

Box 5: Korea

Electronics Technology Project
Project Approve: 1979; Project Completed: 1986, Total amount: US$29 million

The project supported setting up and development of Korean Institute of Electronics Technology (KIET). The project was to support KIET as a central facility in semiconductor industry, including explore and develop export opportunities for Korean electronics sector overseas. The project played a catalytic role in building electronics sector in Korea. However, the project did not meet some of the objectives including profitability targets and industry related R&D programs due to the situation in the country when the industry itself started to invest heavily into semiconductors research leaving less room for KIET, and other economic and business conditions in Korea.

Technology Development Projects (First, Second, and Third)
Projects approved: 1982, 1984, 1988. Projects completed: 1986, 1989, 1992. Total loan amount: US$129 million

The Technology Development Projects were a series of projects designed to foster the technological development of industry in the Republic of Korea through the financing of the Korea Technology Development Corporation (KTDC) and the strengthening of three key institutions: KIST, one of Korea's leading multidisciplinary research institutes; KSBC, the Korea Basic Science Center Support to KIST was intended to cover a broad spectrum of applied research activities and to recruit high-quality researchers; KBSC was established to provide more opportunities for joint basic science research, the foundation of technological innovation; and the role of NITI was to support SMEs by raising product quality. KTDC helped create linkages between the R&D institutes and industry, supported SMEs through the financing of technology start-ups and technological support, and formulated technology policy and appraised national joint R&D projects between SMEs and industry.

Technology Advancement Projects (First, Second, and Third)
Projects approved: 1989, 1990, 1991. Projects completed: 1993, 1994, 1994. Total loan amount: US$108 million

The Technology Advancement projects were a series of projects aimed at providing funds for the purchase of modern equipment for the five main national RDIs. The broad objective of this initiative was to strengthen industrial R&D and basic research capacity and to increase the use of industrial standards in order to raise product quality. These objectives were in conformity with government policy, which sought to expand and strengthen vocational, technical, and tertiary education in science and engineering and to support public and private R&D activities as Korea sought to join the ranks of the industrialized countries. The availability of the new equipment and facilities made it possible for the RDIs to increase their R&D activities and joint projects, expand their testing for quality improvements, and increase their output of technical and scientific publications.

Program for Science and Technical Education Project, Universities Science and Technology Research Project, Science Education and Libraries Computerization Project
Projects approved: 1984, 1990, 1992. Projects completed: 1989, 1995, 1997. Total loan amount: US$195 million

The Program for Science and Technical Education aimed to raise the quality of S&T education to the level required by an industrial system that sought to be more skill- and knowledge-intensive and that was moving toward the use of more advanced technologies. The Universities Science and Technology Research Project aimed to help selected universities strengthen their ability to undertake research in science and technology and strengthen their science teacher education, with the goal of raising the quality of science education in secondary schools. The Science Education and Libraries Computerization Project aimed to help improve the quality of basic science education and to provide a more effective flow of information between those university libraries that service teaching and research.

Intellectual Property Rights Regimes. The prevailing intellectual property rights regime is an important determinant of the amount and quality of technology transfer from industrialized to developing countries as well as development of new ideas in the domestic markets. International evidence suggests that the ease with which foreign companies sell technology to developing countries, the terms on which it is sold (licensed), and the vintage that is sold is affected by the owner's ability to maintain proprietary ownership. As a country moves from importing technology to finding ways of adapting and modifying that technology to serve local demand or technical conditions, the absence of a regime to protect such new ideas additionally can discourage the local developer from investing in its ideas. Knowledge-based societies pay special attention to these issues (for example, the United States is rated as number one in the world by number of patents filed, Japan second, and Taiwan third), while in many developing countries there is a clear failure to understand the importance of these services. The lack of attorneys, patent agents, and judges able to handle infringement cases can mean that the enforcement mechanism for IPR is incapable of playing its role in supporting innovation and technology transfer.

Once other components of innovation systems take hold (such as RDIs reorienting toward applied research, spin-off companies starting to appear in larger quantities, technology financing taking off, and synergies building up between the research community and industry) the question of appropriate support of their IPR becomes even more urgent. Most of these activities inevitably will trigger patenting and licensing disputes if the framework is not functioning properly. (See Box 6.)

Many Bank projects have included intellectual property rights protection in one form or another, from the setting up or upgrading of national-level Patent Offices to the establishment of individual IPR units in universities or R&D Institutions to support the needs of research communities at the micro level. The Turkey Industrial Technology Project, for example, supports modernization of the Turkish IPR regime to align it with the World Trade Organization and European Customs Union requirements. The program stipulates giving assistance to the Turkish Patent Institute in its efforts to upgrade its organizational and operational systems and its physical infrastructure and staff skills, in order to improve the quality and speed of its IPR-related services (such as the issuing of patents, licensing, enforcement, and dissemination of information) and thereby to serve the needs of the industry and research community. The project also supports a promotion campaign, and the training of IPR lawyers, judges, and industry personnel. The ultimate objectives of the intervention in this area are to promote awareness of the IPR regime across the industry and among researchers, to encourage its use by making it more client-oriented and efficient, and ultimately to establish it as a necessary step in the commercialization process. The Mexico Science and Technology Infrastructure Project supported the creation of the Mexican Institute of Industrial Property, significantly reducing delays in the award of patents, increasing enforcement activities, and increasing the number and frequency of inspections related to IPR violations.

Research and Development Institutions. The R&D sector in many developing countries typically comprises a large number of public institutions and universities, in some cases, such as in Russia and Croatia, with an excellent academic base. These institutions tend to be inward-focused, pursuing activities largely disconnected from the needs of industry and the economy at large, and therefore are incapable of serving as effective agents of technology transfer to the private sector. Normally the largest RDIs are and would remain mostly public given their importance for the economy at large and spill-over effects make this public investment into them justified. Returns on the R&D restructuring for the country could be as high as 50 to 100 percent. In Taiwan, for example, the Government set up a public R&D Institute which has resulted in spinning off of two major foundries dealing with semiconductor equipment which in its turn produced linkages with 20,000 small and medium enterprises in the country. In the United States, such examples include National Aeronautics and Space Administration and National Institutes of Health that are publicly funded and provide very strong spill-over effects to the economy. Other examples include India and Korea.

Most S&T projects consequently aim to strengthen and restructure public Research and Development Institutions to serve the economy, to undertake more applied research, and to promote the

Box 6: Turkey

Technology Development Project

Project approved: May 1992. Project completed: June 1998. Loan amount: US$100 million

This project had three broad objectives: (a) to develop the MSTQ system; (b) to encourage market-oriented R&D in the private sector; and (c) to foster the growth of a VC industry. The project supported the establishment of an independent National Metrology Institute (UME), separating it from the Marmara Research Center. By the end of the project UME was able to meet 30–40 percent of the needs of Turkish industry. The project supported modernization of the Turkish Standards Institute and improvement of the standardization processes; it also initiated an R&D financing culture in Turkey by setting up the Technology Development Foundation of Turkey, TTGV, a private sector-managed NGO, and by funding the country's first technology financing program (103 R&D projects financed). However, a VC industry did not materialize due to a range of reasons, including the absence of necessary incentives for the private sector and a lack of support from the International Finance Corporation (IFC), which initially had been nominated as the main catalyst for this effort. The VC component was picked up by the follow-up project.

Industrial Technology Project

Project approved: June 1999. Planned completion: December 2004. Loan amount: US$155 million

The main project objectives are to: (a) assist in the harmonization of Turkish technology infrastructure with ECU standards, and (b) assist firms in upgrading their technological capabilities to improve the competitiveness of Turkish industry. To achieve these objectives, the project concentrated on four main areas: (a) strengthening of IPR services; (b) strengthening of metrology services to serve a larger section of Turkish industry; (c) restructuring of RDIs to make them more industry-oriented; and (d) supporting technology upgrading by firms (including the formation of a VC industry and the establishment of technoparks).

The project follows up on the First Technology Development Project by continuing support to (i) UME, that is developing into a world-class metrology institution capable of meeting 95 percent of Turkish industry's metrology needs, and (ii) the Technology Development Foundation of Turkey that is developing into a diverse technology financing institution that has changed the entire technology financing culture in Turkey. In addition, the Project supports (i) restructuring the public R&D system in Turkey through reconfiguration of Marmara Research Center (MAM, a group of eight leading RDIs), and (ii) upgrading Turkish Intellectual Property Rights (IPR) regime through strengthening Turkish Patent Institute (TPE). As a result of the project investments, by end-2003: (i) UME is capable to meet 80% of the industry's metrology needs and provides about 500 services to the industry; (i) TTGV, in addition to its original technology financing mandate (it has financed some 200 projects to date), has become a catalyst in supporting VC funds (two VCCs were set up with TTGV's equity participation) and also supports two technoparks, in addition, its competitive Technology Support Services (TSS) grant scheme for advisory services has benefited about 600 SMEs; most of TTGV's projects have resulted in the commercialization of R&D outputs; (iii) MAM has increased its contractual research base and industry outreach, and was about 49 percent self-sufficient in 2003, targeting 65–70 percent self-sufficiency by 2006; and (iv) the IPR regime is improving its alignment with ECU and WTO requirements and TPE is developing into an international-level institution.

Knowledge and Innovation Project

Under preparation (2005). Loan amount: US$100 million

This project is expected to focus on a broad KE agenda, building on the two previous projects and the recently completed Knowledge Economy Assessment Study (KEAS). This Study discussed Turkey in the framework of the 4 pillars of the Knowledge Economy and provides key reforms and recommendations in each pillar. Building on these recommendations a new project is under preparation which will focus on the larger KE agenda and build on the successful experience and institutions of the previous two Technology Projects in Turkey. The main components in this project will include: (i) Support to Enterprise Innovation; (ii) Information Society Development; and (iii) Developing Skills for the Knowledge Economy through training to enterprises.

commercialization of their research outputs. The reorientation of S&T to meet industry needs should improve the competitiveness of industry at home and overseas, enhancing the efficiency and quality of research, increasing the synergy between the R&D community and industry, and reducing the burden on public budgets. The objective of such effort is ultimately to make a shift in thinking so that Research *and* Development transforms into Research *for* Development, where "*R*" becomes socially meaningful when it leads to "*D*" and when output is inducted into socioeconomic system. The support given by Bank programs to RDIs includes assistance in the upgrading of physical infrastructure, in the improvement of management information systems and cost accounting systems, and in the modernizing of human resource management and business processes. For greater sustainability, aid also should focus on improving the framework and providing appropriate incentives for cooperation between the research community and industry, by enhancing the incentives for applied research, improving the marketing and commercialization functions of RDIs, introducing competitive research programs, promoting joint projects with industry and other R&D organizations, and introducing a strategic approach to the commercialization of R&D outputs.

Because this restructuring is dynamic in nature and strongly depends on the market and on macro conditions, the strategic approach works best, with R&D Institutions making the difficult and initial decisions first, taking the steps based on the strategy, and where necessary revisiting or

---

BOX 7: CHINA

Rural Industrial Technology (Spark) Project
Project completed: December 1997. Loan amount: US$114 million

The Ministry of Science and Technology's pilot Spark program became nationwide in 1986. The overall objective of the program was to help transfer technological and managerial knowledge from the more advanced sectors of the economy to rural enterprises to support growth and development in the nonstate rural enterprise sector, mostly town and village enterprises, and to help increase output and employment. This project was the first Bank Group-supported operation in China specifically oriented to the rural nonstate industry. The term "Spark" referenced the phrase "one small spark can start a prairie fire," reflecting the anticipated catalytic effect of the program on rural enterprise development.

Technology Development Project
Project approved: 1995. Loan amount: US$200 million

The objective of this project is to support government reforms in technology policy and institutions, with the aim of promoting the development of clean, productivity-enhancing technologies in China's industries. The project is designed to accelerate the diffusion and adaptation of technologies in China and abroad through the deepening of technology markets and through institutional initiatives. The project consists of two components. The first component is designed to assist in transforming part of the R&D establishment into market-responsive technology development corporations. This component will hive off the most dynamic technology development and service-oriented elements of existing research institutions to create, through a competitive selection process, market-oriented Engineering Research Centers. The second component comprises complementary investments aimed at improving public technology services, including the modernization of the National Institute of Metrology and a technical assistance program for a productivity center.

"China and the Knowledge Economy" Report—year 2000
At the request of the Chinese Government, the World Bank Institute conducted a Knowledge Economy Assessment in China, in 2000 publishing "China's Development Strategy: the Knowledge and Innovation Perspective, the World Bank, Washington D.C., 2000 (This report was used by the government as an input into the development of China's 10th Five-Year Plan.) This assessment concluded that China's strategy should be to build a foundation for a knowledge-based economy by (a) updating the economic and institutional regime; (b) upgrading education and learning; (c) building the information infrastructure and raising the technological level of the economy through the active diffusion of new technologies; (d) improving the R&D system; and (e) exploiting global knowledge.

revising the steps as the project progresses. This approach was successfully used in Turkey's Industrial Technology, in which the Marmara Research Center (MAM) and other project agencies prepared medium-term business plans, with a three-year horizon, updating and refining those plans each year as changing conditions required. MAM, the largest RDI in Turkey, comprising eight individual R&D institutes, through support from the World Bank's Industrial Technology Project has restructured itself by modernizing its business processes, downsizing/closing down low-demand areas, transferring one of the institutes to the private sector, reorienting its outputs towards market needs, expanding in areas with the strong prospects, and reducing overhead costs. The center also established a Technopark to promote commercialization of research outputs and to increase cooperation with the private sector. This restructuring has resulted in a significant shift to serve the industry needs in Turkey and also collaborate in the European market. In 2003, MAM covered about 49 percent of its expenses through contractual research (self-sufficiency ratio is 57 percent taking into account interest earned on these funds), and aims to reach 70 percent self-sufficiency by 2006. An earlier Bank project in Mexico linked the investment made in selected R&D institutes with their partial privatization—a unique approach in restructuring that met with mixed results.

The India Industrial Technology Project also supported the restructuring of the largest network of public industrial research and development institutes (38 R&D Laboratories) of the Council for Scientific and Industrial Research (CSIR). As a result of the restructuring, CSIR has more than doubled its share of contractual research to industry (albeit from a low starting level). The CSIR laboratories have undergone a major cultural change, moving to proactive management in public R&D applied research and earning money from industry, foreign clients (CSIR has over 40 agreements with foreign countries, including UK, USA, France, Russia), and international patents (in 2002 CSIR filed 580 patent applications abroad and held 340 active patents abroad). Building up on the project accomplishments, India was able to attract large research contracts from outside of the country (for example, the largest General Electric R&D center outside of the United States is located in India and employs about 1,600 people). Increase in applied research in India also gave boost to the biotechnology revolution resulting in India now holding a prominent place worldwide (the United States holding the first) in the biotechnology area. In the information technologies (IT) area, initially there was no attempt by the Government or the World Bank to promote the regional development of IT in India. Rather, the combination of promotion of excellent higher level education (plus a high level of investment R&D in defense and space) in certain areas as well as the willingness of the government to permit liberalized captive satellite communications by companies exporting IT services and products led to this revolution. Later on financing played a role. This illustrates the importance of governments to be reform minded and find ways to encourage nascent developments be they foreign investment or by local techno-entrepreneurs.

Upgrading enterprise-level innovation capabilities. As seen from Figure 2, in developed countries the bulk of R&D activities are undertaken by business enterprises (OECD 2003). Having established the infrastructure to develop new ideas, it is therefore important that a working framework, capable of supporting the establishment and development of knowledge-based companies, be built to take these ideas further. (Some of these companies will be spin-offs from RDIs or joint projects with the industry while others will emerge through the efforts of entrepreneurial individuals.) The framework should encourage adoption of the new ideas and technologies by industry. Most SMEs are technologically behind the leading edge and need help in acquiring even existing technologies and in adapting existing processes and materials to suit local requirements. To integrate the support available to these companies a country needs to develop functions that can effectively: (a) institutions, starting technology financing programs, or setting up a VC industry); (b) set up and launch knowledge-based companies (through setting up and upgrading the services of incubators and technology and R&D centers); and (c) help existing companies upgrade their capabilities and the quality of their services and products through the acquisition of new technologies (for example, through matching grants schemes and, again, by upgrading technology and R&D centers). The creation of a sound business environment conducive to growth, an increased technological base, and the encouragement of the

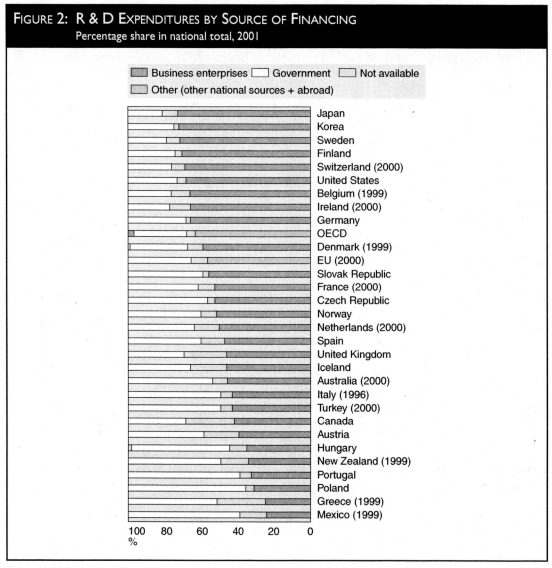

FIGURE 2: R & D EXPENDITURES BY SOURCE OF FINANCING
Percentage share in national total, 2001

Business enterprises ▢ Government ▢ Not available
▢ Other (other national sources + abroad)

Japan
Korea
Sweden
Finland
Switzerland (2000)
United States
Belgium (1999)
Ireland (2000)
Germany
OECD
Denmark (1999)
EU (2000)
Slovak Republic
France (2000)
Czech Republic
Norway
Netherlands (2000)
Spain
United Kingdom
Iceland
Australia (2000)
Italy (1996)
Turkey (2000)
Canada
Austria
Hungary
New Zealand (1999)
Portugal
Poland
Greece (1999)
Mexico (1999)

100   80   60   40   20   0
%

Source: OECD, Science, Technology and Industry Scorecard 2003. Copyright OECD 2003.
http://www1.oecd.org/publications/e-book/92-2003-04-1-7294/pdf/A3.pdf

practical application of technical skills can help companies compete more effectively and can thereby facilitate their economic integration with global markets. The sections below examine in more detail the provision of firm-level assistance.

Financing R&D Development and its Use by Industry

Given the importance of technology development for the economy and its complexity, many countries have set up specialized institutions focusing on technology development financing. As practice shows, governments seldom are equipped to undertake this function and the private sector typically is less than enthusiastic about venturing into it, especially during the early stages of development when the risks involved are high. These technology financing institutions typically are public or public–private partnerships or publicly funded not-for-profit organizations. In addition to their regular business of providing technology financing for individual projects, they also in many cases serve as catalysts for development in new areas, such as venture capital funds, and start-up funds, and

---

Box 8: Chile

Millennium Science Initiative
Project dates: 1999–2002. Loan amount: US$5 million

This project consisted of three components, aimed at creating: (a) a management structure for Millennium Science Initiative; (b) a competitive fund for scientific excellence; and (c) a network for the promotion of scientific excellence.

Science for the Knowledge Economy (Phase I)
Project planned: 2003–2007. Loan amount: US$25 million

Given the long-term commitment that is necessary to consolidate institutional and behavioral changes in the S&T sector, a program approach is proposed for Chile that would use the Adaptable Program Lending (APL) instrument. The program comprises two phases. The first phase, Science for the Knowledge Economy, extends until 2007 and supports the establishment of a strong policy framework. It also will provide for the continuation of the Millennium Science Initiative and a further strengthening of the science base. The second phase (2007–2010) will continue the activities to strengthen Chile's science base, with a view particularly to enhancing private sector R&D. A further phase aimed at improving the innovation system is planned for fiscal 2006.

---

technoparks. The financing provided through such institutions, given its developmental connotation, is typically low-interest, and in some cases is provided in the form of matching grants. The financial instruments employed by technology financing institutions include loans (zero-interest, low-interest, commercial, and conditional), grants (usually competitive matching grants), equity participation (sometimes through venture capital programs), royalties, and guarantees. These matching grant schemes have met with success in several countries including the SPREAD program supported by the India Technology Development Project. This program provided assistance to SMEs to collaborate with Technology Institutions. One start-up, a biotech firm, received SPREAD assistance in 1995, to develop the hepatitis B vaccine in cooperation with the Council for Science and Industrial Research. The company developed the vaccine and began commercial production two years later, resulting in a sharp price decrease for the vaccine. This led to a saving in foreign exchange for a country that had to import the vaccine in large amounts and now has its own production capacity. Examples of technology financing institutions and programs in the industrialized countries include Finland's TEKES, VINNOVA of Sweden, and the Vienna Science and Technology Fund of Austria.

In Turkey, the Bank supported the establishment of the Technology Development Foundation of Turkey (TTGV) as part of the first Technology Development Project. The TTGV initially focused solely on technology development financing to private enterprises developing R&D products, but with the follow-up efforts of the Industrial Technology Project has benefited some 200 companies and is now also involved in two venture capital funds, two technoparks, two innovations centers, and in a start-up fund (to focus on start-up firms and their initial projects). TTGV has also been successful with its matching grants scheme for technical assistance, and has supported more than 600 SMEs in carrying out activities to improve quality and their technology base.

Firm-level technology financing ranges from the provision of seed money for prototype development and the exploration of new business ideas to the support of the commercialization of research outputs. In Turkey, all of these activities were supported under the technology development financing program, but they may also be split into separate programs, as happened in Croatia, which supports prototype development under the TEST Program and prototype commercialization under the RAZUM Program. Experience in implementing these programs worldwide demonstrates the importance of ensuring that from the start they have appropriate guidelines, transparent review procedures, and intellectual property rights-related procedures, and that they make available diverse financial instruments depending upon market requirements.

Another aspect of technology financing, the importation of ideas, was supported in the India Industrial Technology Project, in which one component enabled a wide range of technologies in

BOX 9: MEXICO

Industrial Technology Development Project

Project approved: July 1986. Project completed: June 1993. Loan amount: US$48 million

The project was designed to improve the capability of industry (especially private firms) to undertake the technological innovation needed to contend with the increasing competition that was expected due to the government's economic liberalization program. This project may have been premature, coming as it did in the early stages of what has been a profound transformation of Mexico's economy: conditions were not yet suited for private sector R&D and Mexico was going through one of its worst economic crises. The project nonetheless can be credited for having been a catalyst in the policy dialogue on project and a factor in the ensuing changes in institutions and operational environment that are now providing a much more fertile ground for technological innovation. Studies financed under the project enabled the government to improve its project policy and infrastructure; the metrology studies additionally produced a number of significant findings on which the follow-up project was able to build.

Science and Technology Infrastructure Project

Project approved: May 1992. Project completed: June 1998. Loan amount: US$189 million

The main objectives of this project were to rationalize public sector funding for S&T and to develop technology institutions by supporting the restructuring of a science research program and improving the efficiency of public support. The project was successful in increasing the number of Mexican scientific research publications and their impact, significantly increasing the production of research-trained personnel, renewing the Mexican research instrumentation infrastructure, institutionalizing a merit-based peer review, and improving the efficiency of the National Science and Technology Council. The project supported the creation of the Mexican National Center for Metrology (CENAM), which now has 104 laboratories operational and which has helped to attract foreign investment and promote competitiveness in Mexican industry, and supported the creation of the Mexican Institute of Industrial Property, significantly reducing delays in the award of patents, increasing enforcement activities, and increasing inspections relating to IPR violations. The project was also successful in creating a supply of basic S&T infrastructure and in helping to sustain development of an R&D capacity.

Knowledge Innovation Project

Project approved: June 1998. Project completion expected June 2003. Loan amount: US$300 million

The Knowledge and Innovation Project, approved in 1998 to support a third generation of reforms and to address some of the gaps remaining on completion of the S&T Infrastructure Project. Specifically, it was designed to enhance the effectiveness of research support programs while increasing linkages to user groups in society and industry. The project's development objectives were: (a) to support S&T research by stimulating work in new and lagging fields, specifically by promoting quality in research, by consolidating and improving peer review, and by prioritizing the integration of young researchers into the system; and by overseeing the institutional strengthening of the scientific management research conducted by National Council of Science and Technology (CONACYT); (b) to support joint action between universities/public research institutes and the private sector, by restructuring public S&T institutes to increase cost recovery and reorientation to industry and by matching grants for joint industry-academia projects; and (c) to support the productivity and competitiveness of firms, particularly SMEs, through a technology modernization program to support upgrading with matching grants and through the development of private regional/sectoral institutional technology support centers.

diverse sectors to be imported by firms of all sizes. The project came in at a time when foreign exchange limitations in the country were severe and the rules for the import of technology highly bureaucratic. By supporting this component, the project was not only able to upgrade the technological capacity of firms but was able also to bolster the speed of liberalization. The Mexico and Republic of Korea projects focused on financing to improve the absorption of foreign technology and the commercialization of local technologies. Korean firms, through a series of technology advancement and technology development projects, imported technology in the form of equipment and licenses and depended little on foreign direct investment. The expectation was that firms should become export-oriented soon after entering production, creating a pressure that, combined with policies to encourage industry to enter complex technological areas, encouraged firms to improve their R&D capacity to sustain global competitiveness.

Venture capital. Venture capital plays an important role in the promotion of innovation and launch of knowledge-based companies (OECD 2003, see Figure 3). Traditional financial institutions consider R&D activities a high-risk investment, as most new entrepreneurs lack track record and the conventional collateral and equity resources. There is a need therefore for non-traditional financial instruments that are not based on conventional commercial terms and collateral requirements, to support innovative ideas. Venture capitalists can fill this gap and more, as they typically do not just provide funding but also know-how, advice, and "hand-holding" services. This specialized form of financial service is based on a deep knowledge of the innovations sector, and can be very rewarding for the investor. However, in many countries Venture Capital Funds (VCFs) have proven risk-averse, focusing on the expansion of businesses in general rather than on R&D-driven new ideas. The Bank has been instrumental in many cases in creating or realigning a VC industry to support also grassroots activities. This venture capital culture needs to be promoted to attract the right kind of investors and the skills needed to run risky, but rewarding, operations.

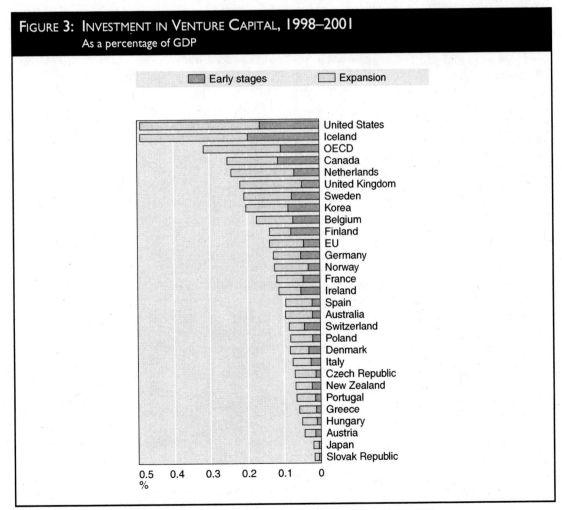

FIGURE 3: INVESTMENT IN VENTURE CAPITAL, 1998–2001
As a percentage of GDP

Source: OECD, Science, Technology and Industry Scorecard 2003. Copyright OECD 2003.
http://www1.oecd.org/publications/e-book/92-2003-04-1-7294/pdf/A7.pdf

There is some debate in the system about the utility of VCFs and their impact on the development of a sound market for technological ideas. There also is a concern that government participation in what is primarily a private-sector endeavor may not be welcome, raising as it does the fear of political interference in business decisions. Research indicates, however, that a properly set-up venture capital industry, supported with public funds, can make a useful contribution to the development of technology financing and the creation of knowledge-based companies. In Israel, Government's support of new R&D projects through venture capital (YOZMA Programs[3]) combined with the immigration of skilled and knowledgeable workers from Russia produced an exceptionally good effect for the economy. Since inception in 1993, YOZMA managed more than $170 million and has made direct investments in more than 40 portfolio companies as well as helping a significant number of its portfolio companies go public on major stock exchanges in the US and Europe. The YOZMA funds were instrumental in positioning the portfolio companies for acquisition or an investment by leading corporations such as Agilent, America On Line, Cisco, Computer Associates, ECI Telecom, Enron, General Instruments, Johnson & Johnson, Medtronic, Microsoft, Sequoia Capital and Terayon.

In collaboration with capital markets boards, the Bank has used awareness-raising and demand-assessment seminars to facilitate the formation of venture capital funds. The approach used has been to encourage minority equity participation in the high-tech sector, through funds that are then managed and operated by the private sector. This practice has proved successful in India, Turkey, and Israel, among others. In India, the Industrial Technology Project supported six Venture Capital Companies (VCCs) involving nine funds. These VCCs have invested in more than 300 companies, producing average returns of 18–20 percent—a performance that is considerably better than that of most venture capital activities in infancy. The project in essence launched the venture capital industry in India by building upon the existence of one entity and encouraging the framing of appropriate policies and incentives. Its contribution, in terms of influencing the culture of risk finance and enabling foreign venture capitalists to be attracted to India, was equally if not more important than its dollar contribution. In Turkey, the Industrial Technology Project similarly has supported two venture capital funds jointly with Turkish and international investors, including the International Finance Corporation and European Investors.

Technical assistance grants for productivity and quality enhancement. To offset the learning costs of firms during the initial acquisition of technology services, and to promote technology diffusion through strong demonstration effects, countries establish specialized facilities to provide matching grants to individual firms for technical assistance to enhance productivity and quality. Through these programs firms receive technical assistance and training to improve their technical processes, marketing, and financial management, to acquire clean technologies, to diversify production, and so forth. Indirectly, these programs also support the development of a domestic consulting market for technology and business services. One successful example is the Turkey Technology Support Services (TSS) Program, and a Productivity and Quality Facility (PQF) is also being set up in Croatia. The PQF, similarly to the TSS, will focus on providing rapid support to firms in relatively simple activities related to productivity and quality enhancement. Other examples of matching grant schemes include Indonesia's Industrial Technology Development Project and Mexico's Knowledge and Innovation Project.

Technoparks, science parks, and technology and R&D centers. The primary contribution of support entities such as technoparks is in helping the development of the local R&D industry and improving the linkages between the research and industry communities. These entities normally are built as a

---

[3]Yozma has earned worldwide recognition as the creator of the Israeli venture capital industry to support R&D and its commercialization. Yozma makes equity investments in technology companies engaged in fields where Israel has demonstrated world leadership. The Group targets high-growth companies in the sectors of communications, information technologies and life sciences.

result of local initiatives to support firm-level innovation and technology development and to improve the use, adaptation, development, and commercialization of new technologies. In addition to the obvious benefits of profit generation for the entity housing a technopark and of the support they give to local business development, many see these initiatives as important means by which research and development institutions and universities can commercialize their own ideas.

Technoparks focus on technology-intensive development, generally with a university or research institution as a key part of their establishment and operation. The university or research institution can contribute faculty members, students, libraries, laboratories, technological infrastructure to the overall operation; the technopark itself typically is characterized by the presence of large, mature tenants that can make the substantial commitment required to take advantage of the academic or research potential of the nearby institution. Technopark investments are typically considered to be of a high-risk and high-reward nature, and thus typically are piloted in a phased manner on the basis of well-defined business plans and entry and exit criteria for the tenant firms. The Turkey Industrial Technology Project is supporting three technoparks and two innovation centers; other successful parks can be found in Israel and throughout Europe, in the United Kingdom, Finland, Spain, Taiwan, and Ireland, for example.

Science parks are similar establishments, but are usually smaller and focus more on incubator-type activities. Otherwise they share many of the characteristics of a technopark, commonly being based on an RDI or university and building on the potential of the linkages between the research staff and tenant firms. Technology centers and incubators provide a complementary service, usually in the form of advisory services for SMEs seeking to develop new technologies. These centers also provide infrastructural support to firms, and are an effective tool in addressing the local and regional needs of industry and in assisting local start-up companies. One example, Armenia's Enterprise Incubator Project, initiated in 2002, aims to create business services centers to promote the Armenian IT industry to potential investors and business partners. It has thus far had limited success, however, as the project design is complex and the implementing institutions are still building capacity, and as a result have had difficulty meeting the requirements needed for broader Armenian reforms.

Education and Lifelong Learning

As mentioned earlier, Bank experience in building the four pillars of the knowledge economy has been most substantial in the areas of innovation systems and policy framework. It is important for context however, to provide at least a brief discussion of the other two areas: education and training, and the information infrastructure.

Equipping people to deal with the demands of knowledge-based economic growth requires a new model of education and training, with an emphasis on lifelong learning. A lifelong learning framework encompasses learning throughout the lifecycle, from early childhood through retirement. It encompasses formal learning (provided by schools, training institutions, and universities), non-formal learning (such as structured, on-the-job training), and informal learning (skills learned from family members or people in the community). It allows people to access learning opportunities, as they need them rather than because they have reached a certain age. Lifelong learning is crucial for preparing workers to compete in the global economy, but it is important for other reasons as well: by improving people's ability to function as members of their economy, for example, it increases social cohesion and improves income distribution. Developing countries and countries in transition risk being further marginalized in a competitive global knowledge economy if their education and training systems fail to equip learners with the skills they need (World Bank 2003). In response to this problem, in recent decades the Bank has launched several projects designed to equip a country's labor force to adapt to the changing needs of the global market.

General reforms in this sector have included the modernization of teaching curricula and of the testing and examination process, with the aims of helping industry meet international standards, assisting in the creation of qualification assurance systems to certify the competencies of individuals and accredit firms and institutions, and meeting the training needs of industry. Critically, the reforms have sought to establish new mechanisms by which to finance education and to improve access to learning services.

Formal learning. The Bank has been engaged in a number of projects in the primary and secondary education areas to improve science and math skills, to modernize curricula to international standards, and to introduce more ICT components into basic education. Of these, this paper focuses on those projects targeted at higher education, specifically at the university and graduate level. There have been significant investments in this area by many countries. Projects in science and technology, even those launched prior to the last decade, have made significant investments in upgrading science, engineering, and technical skills. This is partially due to the emphasis that countries have made on the input parameters of the innovation system, which has guided the effort to upgrade the number and capabilities of scientists and researchers. Examples of such projects have included the Science and Technical Education project in the Republic of Korea, designed to improve the quality of science and technical education and research; the Science Education and Libraries Computerization Project, in the same country, to improve the quality of basic science education and to provide a more effective flow of information between the university libraries that service teaching and research; the Philippines Engineering and Science Education Project, aimed at upgrading the country's industrial and technological capability by increasing the supply of high-level S&T manpower; Tunisia's Higher Education Restructuring Project, designed to make the higher education system more responsive to the country's needs and to improve its performance in economic terms (cost effectiveness) and human terms (the proportion of university entrants who successfully graduate); the India Technical Engineering Quality Improvement Project; and Indonesia's University Research for Graduate Education Project, which aimed to improve the quality of graduate education.

Nonformal learning. The supply-driven model of education emphasizes the production of scientists and researchers, but the increasingly predominant demand-driven model uses industry needs to determine the skills needed in the workplace. According to this model, nonformal, industry-specific training and skill upgrading are a priority. Firms provide this education for their employees at various levels and through diverse programs, and formalizing the private sector participation in this process has become an important item on the education reform agenda. Support programs increasingly are seeking to integrate the education sector into the broader economic growth strategy in an approach that is quite different from the traditional focus of education reform, which has tended to be on education subsectors (higher education, basic education, continuing education, and so on). By structuring the education components of KE programs in this way, the program designers can keep sight of the demand-side requirements of education—that is, the requirements of the economy and of the labor market. Examples include the Indonesia Second Professional Human Resource Development Project, which aimed to upgrade the quality of professional, managerial, and S&T staff in key government ministries and agencies, both at local and national levels and, on a limited scale, in the private sector; the Malaysia Polytechnic Development Project, designed to improve the efficiency and capacity of technical education by establishing training practices that are market-oriented and as such seek to reduce structural unemployment and encourage greater labor absorption and mobility; and the Mauritus Higher and Technical Education Project, aimed to produce personnel trained to support a more competitive economy.

Informal learning. A third area of focus in lifelong learning is that of informal learning, by which workers learn through their communities and family. This is an area in which little work has been done, but the Bank has begun to emphasize this as an additional component when modernizing education systems in developing countries.

Financing of education. The move toward a lifelong learning system can be an expensive one for developing countries. While most education spending is based on local costs, many essential inputs of lifelong learning, such as computers, laboratories, and Internet access, are priced on an international scale. Most of the money that funds education in developing economies comes from public funds, and these funds typically are inadequate to extend education opportunities to everyone. There are several financing instruments that have been used to increase private-sector participation in this arena, however. For example, Mexico's Higher Education Financing Project, which aims to assist academically qualified but economically disadvantaged students to pursue advanced studies, operates a private sector student loan program. Elsewhere, Indonesia's Higher Education Support Project and Romania's Reform of Higher Education and Research Project, completed in 2002, are examples of competitive research programs.

Information Infrastructure (ICT/e-Development)

Information and Communications Technology (ICT). A well-functioning communications infrastructure is the backbone of a knowledge-based economy. Privatization and liberalization are essential for the development of an affordable and modern telecommunications infrastructure. The key areas of focus are: (a) improving universal access to telecom services; (b) promoting affordable Internet access; (c) improving telecom infrastructure in rural areas; and (d) promoting alternative means of communication, such as wireless services. Modern information communications has the potential of eliminating the disadvantages of peripheral location, and as such is an equalizer of opportunities: Internet and mobile communications can help a company anywhere to establish a global presence and communicate on the global scale.

Box 10: IPR Case Study—India National Chemical Laboratory (NCL)

The India Industrial Technology Project began the process of transformation of the Council of Scientific and Industrial Research (CSIR) after nearly a half-century of inertia. CSIR is India's largest R&D network with 40 research laboratories and over 25,000 staff. The project initiated the revamping of this institution through dramatic modernization of business and HR processes, performance and outputs, and a reorientation towards industry through enhanced customer orientation and market responsiveness. This was re-emphasized in their vision and strategy whereby they envisaged:

- re-engineering of the organizational structure to enable CSIR to become more customer oriented;
- linking the R&D programs and activities to the industry through alliances, networking and partnerships;
- stimulating the intellectual property management in CSIR;
- investing in select high quality science that would be the precursor for high-technology; and
- refurbishing human and physical capital.

One example of the momentum achieved by this institution is the specific case of one of its laboratories, NCL. The Bank supported technology project for India had a component of a grant to NCL. Among other things, NCL used this grant to enhance its capacity in intellectual property rights. NCL scientists were sent for training in IPR to British Technology Group in UK. These scientists brought and spread a new culture on patenting in NCL. (Note that the number of US patents granted to NCL till 1989 were zero). NCL acquired a patent on Solid State Polycondensation of Polycarbonate that was licensed to General Electric (GE), who had 40 percent of world market share of polycarbonate. This built the partnership between NCL and GE. It grew to such an extent that Jack Welch, the CEO of General Electric (GE), decided to set up the GE R&D Centre in India. This centre today employs over 1600 people (with further expansion planned to 2400). This is the second largest R&D centre of GE in the world. GE's example was followed by many leading companies. India today is emerging as a global platform for R&D, as many companies are following GE's example. Indeed, over 100 companies have set up their R&D centers in India now. For CSIR's Senior Management, the catalytic effect of the Bank's technology project is clear through this simple example of NCL developing the capacity to file and win US patents which acted as in initial trigger for the NCL-GE partnership and ultimately resulted in GE's decision to set up R&D Centre in Bangalore.

Electronic Development *(e-Development)* applications ease and can make more efficient the transaction process between government, private firms, and civil society. These applications can take many forms:

- *Intragovernment interaction:* Modernizing systems and processes to enhance the communication and information flow within and between ministries and different governmental organizations (for example, e-Budgeting).
- *Government-to-business interaction:* Creating an environment conducive to business, to improve efficiency in public spending and improve transparency (e-Licensing, e-Procurement, e-Registration).
- *Government-to-civil-society interaction:* Expanding access to government information to reduce bureaucracy, inefficiency, and enhance transparency (e-Justice).
- *Business-to-business applications* (e-Commerce, e-Supplier, e-Vendor, e-Services)
- *Business-to-customer applications* (e-Banking, e-Payments)

Major issues to be tackled within the e-Development agenda include contract enforcement, consumer protection, liability assignment, privacy protection, process and technical standards, security, authentication, encryption, digital signatures, and connectivity protocols.

Several Bank projects have addressed e-Development issues in policy reform and the use of ICT. While some projects, like e-Sri-Lanka, take an integrated approach to e-Development by attempting to tackle most of system within one project, most others focus on a small group of related issues at a time and phase the operations based on their readiness. For example, the Venezuela Supreme Court Modernization Project, completed in 1998, supported the tremendous potential of technology-driven reform. By streamlining and automating case handling and reporting systems, the court eliminated multi-year backlogs that had hampered its efficiency and eroded public confidence in the institution.[4] Turkey's recently completed Public Finance Management Project, a state-of-the-art modern budget execution system, successfully deployed the "say 2000i" system, which embodies the functionality of a financial ledger system and has the reporting capabilities and capacity to provide the Ministry of Finance with accurate and timely information on the status of budget execution. A project under preparation in Russia, the Customs Development Project, aims to reform and modernize the Russian Customs administration.

---

[4]See the Venezuela Supreme Court Modernization Project website: http://www.tsj.gov.ve/

CHAPTER 4

MONITORING AND EVALUATION

One of the main characteristics (and a cornerstone of the rationale) of technology support is the public-good nature of technology development and the upgrading that results due to the high spillovers from such efforts. It is difficult to measure these factors in traditional terms, such as net present value or financial rate of return, and it is difficult to make estimations of the benefits that might flow from the proposed investment. At the same time, however, it is imperative that the impact of investments in this area be monitored if private sector involvement is desired. The proposed approach to this dilemma has two components: (a) empirical analysis of the benefits to the economy; and (b) development of a set of project-specific performance indicators capable of measuring progress toward the project's objectives. The project's outcomes analysis should, in addition to project specific indicators, include a broader good for the country such as FDI inflows, international outreach and collaboration of the beneficiaries, employment generation in the country. Surveys and interviews are important tools in assessing technology projects.

Empirical analysis should include benchmark analysis of the economic conditions at the beginning of the project and subsequent analysis (midway through the project and at the end) to check the hypothesis of improved economic conditions. The variables to be examined may include the growth of new business, exports, market share held by R&D companies, company profitability indicators, and, ultimately, such economic indicators as gross domestic product growth, growth in R&D expenditures, and foreign direct investment.

Specific project indicators should be developed at three levels: (a) input indicators to keep track of the extent to which implementation meets the stated expectations and schedule; (b) output indicators to track the immediate results of implementation, in accordance with project plans; and (c) outcome indicators (including development impact indicators) to evaluate the extent to which the project has achieved its objective of improving technology development. Each set of indicators should be supported by specific ratios and measurable data, collected over the project lifetime. For example, input indicators could include the percentage of investments completed, and the number of new laboratories equipped or opened. Output indicators could include progress on the number of patent applications processed (for patent agencies), the average time required for application processing, industrial research income (public and private), industrial contracts income, the number of clients, the number of joint projects, the number of publications, the self-sufficiency ratio, and repayment ratios (in the case of technology financing). Outcome indicators could include increases in the country's R&D expenditure, the improvement in access to financing of technology companies, increases of exports by beneficiary firms, commercialization of new technologies, the reduction of barriers between industry and the research community, and the regional outreach of programs. Performance indicators should measure not only output indicators but also process indicators (restructuring of institutions, business process reengineering, reorienting to industry needs, etc.)

Monitoring and evaluation (M&E) activities are best carried out systematically. Performance indicators should be updated periodically by responsible project agencies during their reporting cycles (at least semiannually), and empirical studies, including surveys and interviews, could be outsourced to private sector firms or statistics institutions. An M&E scheme along these lines was successfully introduced under the Turkey Industrial Technology Project, and is present in various forms of sophistication in several projects.

CHAPTER 5

LESSONS

*P*roject Scope and Complexity. Technology projects normally include a wide spectrum of interventions, all of which are complementary in nature and would not function well without each other. The composition of the project would depend on the country situation and would be unique in each case. On the supply side, the reforms can (a) tackle the restructuring of R&D Institutions to reorient them toward industry; (b) build up a functioning measurements, standards, testing and quality system to improve competitiveness of products domestically and internationally; and (c) provide the necessary protection to the industry in the form of a healthy intellectual property rights regime. On the demand side, the reforms can support the use and adaptation by the industry of innovations and new technologies developed by the research community. It should also be noted that the technology sector cannot function unless appropriate technology financing programs, including venture capital, and start-up funds, are in place.

Technology projects typically are complex, contain multiple components of a complementary character, and must be seen as long-term efforts. Experience has shown that a systemic and holistic approach to technology development works best and that such operations should not be too narrow. Each technology project has to be "custom-designed" and must be a product of a collaborative approach among the stakeholders in the country. A series of projects or an adaptable programmatic lending approach can work well, as this allows a country to develop a long-term strategy, complemented by medium-term interventions. As the examples described in the boxes in this report show, Mexico, Turkey, India, Chile, and many other countries are not only applying a multisectoral approach, wherein different projects look at different sectors and improve them simultaneously, but they are also looking at multigenerational approaches, wherein the vision and strategy is determined with a long horizon and prioritized activities are undertaken in a sequenced approach to meet that vision. Lessons learnt from previous Bank projects endorse this approach by suggesting that technology development be tackled in an integrated way and as part of a broader industrialization strategy. No single project, of course, can or should try to address all issues.

The complementarity of activities and the built-in synergies in these projects imply complexity in design, and as a result these projects are labor-intensive and resource-intensive to prepare and supervise (for both the client and the Bank). The projects require support from the public sector, to promote investment in R&D. Given the difficulties of the initial reforms and delayed return for the economy, the innovation support agenda sometimes is accorded low priority by the busy governments struggling with fiscal deficits and other macro-economic challenges. Therefore, technology projects require strong dedicated championship in the country to move the reforms along on both the Government and the institutional level. The role of a strong local champion is crucial for following through with the tough initial reforms as well as to ensure integrity of the project design for all Bank projects, but even more so for the innovation support ones. The Bank should not launch into extensive project preparation (and ultimately, implementation) without finding such a local champion.

The technology projects also require intensive preparation and supervision by the Bank, and as a result the lending and supervision budgets of these projects are typically higher than average. Continuity in the skilled and dedicated Bank staff managing these projects is also critical to ensure the transfer of knowledge as well as benefit of the worldwide experience. The capacity of the Bank project teams must be increased to allow them to provide high-quality advice and coordination skills to meet the expectations of the highly sophisticated clients in the Innovations Systems area.

Flexibility in project design. Given the nature of technology development activities and the newness of many of these activities in some countries, it is not always appropriate to follow a rigid implementation scenario. It is therefore critical that flexibility be incorporated into the project design, to enhance its effectiveness and to reduce the bureaucracy involved in implementation and to permit adaptation of the project to changes in the institutional and economic environment. This flexibility includes the incorporation of unallocated funds for use in priority activities that demonstrate superior performance, as well as pilot initiatives to determine viability and the annual review and updating of business plans. Intensive monitoring to determine if continuation or modification of project elements is required and to permit a rapid response to changing needs is an integral part of the process. It may also prove beneficial for the projects to focus on the mechanisms and how they work—criteria, transparency, speed, reliability, and oversight–and improve them overtime through effective evaluation processes. A good feedback loop to adjust to changing needs should be incorporated in project design to allow for appropriate and necessary adjustments. This was crucial to the success of the India Industrial Technology Project, the Indonesia Industrial Technology Project and the Turkey Industrial Technology Project. Each of these projects survived well in environments that went through major economic upheavals. However, these projects also succeeded mainly due to strong local ownership and champions, committed institutional leadership and recognition of projects long-term benefits and impact as well as appropriate response by both the Bank and the Government/Institutions in accommodating changing needs during the project lifecycle.

Public-good nature and externalities. Due to the public-good nature of investment in measurements, standards, testing and quality systems and R&D infrastructure and the high spillover effects and externalities associated with the generation, adaptation, and diffusion of new technologies, the involvement of the public sector in this area is justified. The private sector normally would invest in these activities only to the extent that it could internalize the benefits of these investments fully and make a profit. This is possible only for very large firms, leaving a large part of the industry needs unfulfilled and the level of private investment far below the socially optimal level. The role of the public sector therefore is crucial, in its ability to create a shared approach by providing support for the setting-up of technology services where they do not exist or the reorientation of those that do exist. Building a good institutional framework and setting up regulations conducive for technology development remain the responsibility of the public sector. Many MSTQ services, especially metrology services, remain in part publicly funded even after they are up and running, but the cost to the government will be far outweighed by the benefits of a well-running system that accrue for the economy at large.

Private sector participation. Public sector approaches in the past have led to inefficient infrastructure and services that do not respond well to industry needs. An emphasis on private sector participation therefore is important in the restructuring process, for the sector's ability to inject into the process efficiency, management capability, good governance, and cost-effective design and delivery. Cofinancing from the private sector and the setting up of advisory boards and councils with private sector participation, while maintaining involvement of the public sector, have in past experience proved valuable in helping maintain a business focus that benefits the economy. Also, private sector research community involvement in the project evaluation and monitoring process is important.

Venture capital and technoparks initiatives should not even be considered unless there is strong support and cofinancing from the private sector. The Government's role should be restricted to providing seed funds to start and catalyze these initiatives, but they should ultimately be managed by the private sector and funded by other sources (for example, in the India case, 25–33 percent of venture capital funds were financed through the Bank loan, while the Turkey Industrial Technology Project financed 12 percent of the equity participation in individual venture capital funds, and 30 percent in the technoparks).

Technology financing agencies. Some later Bank projects have financed autonomous counterpart technology financing agencies to maximize the ability to achieve project goals and objectives in this area. If they are to be able effectively to take risks and attract high-caliber professionals and entrepreneurs, these intermediary agencies should be set up with independent management, professionalism, and should bring with them knowledge of different industries and the R&D sector. Specialized technology financing agencies are best equipped for lending to technology programs. The Korea, India, and Turkey experiences illustrate the advantages of working with professionally managed institutions that are responsive to market needs.

Institutional reforms. Any effort to change an entrenched mindset will be slow. In this arena typically there will be strong resistance from the research community, which traditionally is focused on academia and publishing. The momentum in these projects usually rises slowly in the initial stages. It is therefore important that incentives, both career and financial, and on the institutional and individual levels, be strong: public institutions should be made accountable for their performance to encourage them to strive for their specific goals, and scientists must be rewarded for initiating joint projects and conducting applied research for industry. The modern business culture and management experience typically are unfamiliar to the scientific community at large, and therefore incentive changes must be combined with training and awareness-building. As the restructuring of public institutions to meet industry needs unavoidably will lead to closures in nonperforming areas and enlargement in promising areas, fully considered and transparent staff redundancy plans need be put in place. The fair and transparent treatment of human resource matters can help smooth the process of reform and reduce the resistance to change; it also can help the public to understand the process and its objectives and thus build up broader support.

Management Intensity. The technology-related business, and specifically projects targeting the restructuring of the technology sector, require high level of management and coordination effort. Such projects are labor- and resource-intensive, and would ideally require the solid commitment of and tough decision-making by government and institutions before the beginning of the project, require a change in the mindset of relevant institutions, and must involve the participation of the private sector, a beast that has a mind of its own and that cannot be lured into doing something that offers no profit or gain. It would be most desirable that the government and key institutions make their tough decisions upfront. Making the key decisions early on the autonomy and governance, and setting up a functioning change management group, will in addition to increasing probability of success of the operation also help to maintain the momentum of the reform. However, in real life one needs to find a reasonable balance between the commitment, reforms and timeliness, and some tough decisions will inevitable be carried out into the implementation period.

Time factor. It is important, finally, to have an end in sight. Typical Bank-loan four-to-five-year time horizon has proven to be effective for successful implementation. Most successful projects do not wait for a country's entire reform process to be either initiated or completed, but work within the existing agenda by phasing reforms and often catalyzing the future steps.

Impediments to Avoid. As mentioned earlier, the Bank can play an important role in assisting client countries in upgrading their innovation systems, including scientific and technological capacity. However, the success level has been mixed. This review of Bank projects, in particular of the factors contributing to their success and failure, has revealed a number of impediments to successful achievement of project objectives. The key impediments on the Bank side include highly complex project design combined with rigidity, inadequate resources for preparation and supervision, poor monitoring and evaluation processes, a lack of continuity and appropriate skills and dedication in project teams to customize project design to country context and local institutional capacity, poor resolve to follow through on institutional and policy issues. On the Client side, the key issues involve weak leadership and institutional capacity, resistance to long-term commitment to change, weak policy framework, a lack of continuity in institutions and in the project management teams, inadequate autonomy and governance structures of the project beneficiaries, a lack of effective monitoring and evaluation systems and lax focus on project impact. Therefore, it is important to ensure that these issues are effectively addressed during the design and implementation stages of these inherently complex and attention intensive but highly rewarding projects.

ANNEXES

KNOWLEDGE ECONOMY PROJECT MENU

Potential Interventions in the Four Pillars of the Knowledge Economy

I Policy and Institutional Framework

    A *An appropriate policy, regulatory, and institutional environment* to promote business investment and economic growth driven by innovation:
- Openness to trade and foreign direct investment
- Credit and financial sector policies to deepen financial intermediation
- Judicial systems to improve the rule of law and its enforcement
- Labor markets to be stimulated to create a supply of knowledge workers (including development of conducive labor codes, redundancy regulations, human resources regulations, and so forth)
- Development of regulations governing distance learning establishments, their accreditation and supervision
- Environment to support public research and development institutions and their staff engaging in contractual research and commercialization of R&D

    B *Domestic competition policy* to promote sustained economic growth and ease the entry and exit of firms into and out of the market:
- Intellectual Property Rights regime to align with World Trade Organization and European Union standards
- National competitiveness policy, including antimonopoly regulations and the setting up and strengthening of antimonopoly institutions
- Science and higher education policy to be aligned with the needs of the economy
- Business environment to be conducive to private sector investment in new technological ventures (including appropriate regulations and incentives for venture capital);

▓ Tax and other incentives to improve private sector participation in R&D, including investment in R&D (adapt, use and develop R&D) and promotion of knowledge-based companies

▓ Privatization and liberalization of telecommunications and postal services

C *Support for technology policy,* through the setting up and/or strengthening of technology policy institutions to enable them (and to finance some of their activities) to carry out adequate policy studies, conducting foresight studies, serve as data centers on technology issues for private and public sectors both locally and internationally, and to carry out technology outreach and public awareness activities.

II Innovation Systems

A *Upgrade intellectual property rights (IPR) regime and metrology, standards, testing, and quality (MSTQ) systems* to enhance the competitiveness of the economy and increase trade by aligning the policy, legal, and institutional framework and physical infrastructure with EU and WTO standards:

▓ Strengthen IPR regime, upgrading the national patent organization's physical infrastructure; improve the quality and speed of services; train patent judges, lawyers, and industry; improve information dissemination

▓ Improve national standard and quality systems by enhancing the role of the private sector in service delivery; upgrading physical and laboratory infrastructure; improving the quality and speed of services; and reducing costs

▓ Upgrade metrology services by strengthening national metrology organizations and private laboratories; upgrading metrology facilities and laboratories; improving the quality, number, and type of services; improving awareness among the industry and academic community; and promoting the systems and training users

▓ Create institutional infrastructure for quality enhancement and certifications, including national quality councils and national accreditation systems

B *Restructure R&D institutions* to improve the efficiency and quality of research, increase the synergy between the R&D community and industry, and reduce the burden on public budgets.

▓ Enhance the benefits of R&D to society by upgrading laboratory facilities and staff skills, modernizing management and HR systems and business processes, improving marketing and commercialization functions, enhancing the incentives for applied research

▓ Introducing competitive research programs

▓ Promote joint projects with industry and other R&D organizations

C *Support firm-level innovation and technology development* to improve the use, adaptation, development, and commercialization of new technologies:

▓ Strengthen technology financing institutions with private sector participation and build their capacity to provide various types of assistance to knowledge-based companies

▓ Introduce appropriate financial products to provide low-interest loans, equity, and matching grants to firms for R&D activities and prototype building and for the commercialization of such ideas

▓ Promote venture capital funds to provide equity financing (and assistance to entrepreneurs): start-up capital funds to focus on new ventures, and technology funds to support the projects of established companies

▓ Provide small matching grants for quick technical assistance support for feasibility studies, quality assessments, international standards certifications, process improvements, and other noncomplex measures to improve the quality of products or processes and to develop new products

- Support technology and science parks, preferably linked in research and development institutions, to help build synergies with industry by bringing together researchers, laboratory facilities, and private firms
- Set up business incubators and technology service centers to encourage technology-focused new entrepreneurship and to encourage local initiatives to promote SME growth by providing fee-based premises, logistical support, and training

III Education and Lifelong Learning

A. *General reforms*

- Modernize the curricula and testing and examination process at all levels to meet the needs of industry and to meet international standards
- Align academic research toward industry needs:
  - Restructure (in some cases establish) education councils and boards to include private sector representatives and sponsors, to ensure alignment with industry needs and to introduce commercial practices
  - Develop the environment and promote informal learning
  - Improve the research base and integrate with the international community through joint collaborations on publications and projects

B. *Qualification assurance and certification*

- Create qualification assurance systems to certify individuals and to accredit institutions and firms
- Design national (unified) testing system for higher education establishments, to provide unified requirements for future students, to make admissions more transparent, and to reduce the cost of the admission process

C. *Specific assistance to meet training needs*

- Provide vocational training through private sector partnerships to meet the demands of the labor market
- Provide retraining for workers to adapt their skills (especially Internet and business and marketing skills) in the rapidly changing environment of the knowledge economy
- Provide training and assistance for redundant employees to reorient them for the job market and to teach new skills
- Provide distance learning (Internet-based education)
- Improve computer literacy and Internet-based skills:
- Start computer (basic programming and software use) training early in schools and continue into adulthood
- Connect schools and universities to the Internet
- Provide vocational information and communications technology (ICT) training
- Provide ICT training to enable civil servants to work effectively with modern systems and processes, including e-applications such as e-Procurement, e-Budgeting, and e-Information.

D. *Education financing products*

- Encourage private-sector-driven financing (scholarships, competitive funds, long-term education loans with income-contingent repayment schemes, and so forth)
- Support the public with subsidies, grants, and targeted education vouchers

IV ICT/e-Development

A. *ICT infrastructure*

- Modernize telecommunications networks
- Promote alternative communication tools (wireless services)

- Improve access to telecommunications (including that of low-income, rural, and other groups—"bridging the digital divide")
- Promote affordable Internet access, especially in rural areas
- Support creation of a global distance learning network

B. *e-Development applications*

- Intragovernmental interaction: Modernize systems and processes to enhance the communication and information flow within and between ministries and different governmental organizations
- e-Budgeting—to enhance efficiency and transparency in public expenditures management
- Government-to-business interaction: Create an environment conducive to business, improve efficiency in public spending, and improve transparency
- e-Registration—to reduce the time taken for and costs of the SME registration process
- e-Procurement—to reduce costs, strengthen competition, and enhance transparency and thereby to support the participation of SMEs in the public procurement process;
- e-Taxation—to improve revenue collection, enhance transparency, and increase efficiency of the public tax system
- digital signatures—to enhance the speed of B2B transactions and improve the efficiency of business contracting
- e-Credit information system—to improve the availability to financial institutions of the credit history of borrowers and thereby to enhance the access to finance of SMEs
- e-Mortgage and pledge registry (of fixed and movable assets)—to improve creditor rights and thereby to enhance financial intermediation in the economy
- e-Investor—to improve the foreign direct investment flow in the economy by serving as the first point of contact for investors, especially foreign
- Government-to-civil-society interaction: Expand access to government information to reduce bureaucracy and inefficiency and to enhance transparency
- e-Justice—to streamline and automate case handling and reporting systems, and thereby to reduce multi-year backlogs and improve the efficiency of the courts
- e-Health—to provide access for service providers to vital information and statistics, and thereby to enhance service delivery
- Land Cadastre—to improve access to land records and titles information, to develop land markets and improve financial intermediation
- Business-to-business applications
- e-Commerce
- Data and information exchange tools for business
- Business-to-client applications
- e-Services
- e-Payments (bills, taxes, and so forth)

V Education and Lifelong Learning

A. *General reforms*

- Modernize the curricula and testing and examination process at all levels to meet the needs of industry and to meet international standards
- Align academic research toward industry needs:
  - Restructure (in some cases establish) education councils and boards to include private sector representatives and sponsors, to ensure alignment with industry needs and to introduce commercial practices
  - Develop the environment and promote informal learning
  - Improve the research base and integrate with the international community through joint collaborations on publications and projects

B. *Qualification assurance and certification*
- Create qualification assurance systems to certify individuals and to accredit institutions and firms
- Design national (unified) testing system for higher education establishments, to provide unified requirements for future students, to make admissions more transparent, and to reduce the cost of the admission process

C. *Specific assistance to meet training needs*
- Provide vocational training through private sector partnerships to meet the demands of the labor market
- Provide retraining for workers to adapt their skills (especially Internet and business and marketing skills) in the rapidly changing environment of the knowledge economy
- Provide training and assistance for redundant employees to reorient them for the job market and to teach new skills
- Provide distance learning (Internet-based education)
- Improve computer literacy and Internet-based skills:
  - Start computer (basic programming and software use) training early in schools and continue into adulthood
  - Connect schools and universities to the Internet
  - Provide vocational information and communications technology (ICT) training
  - Provide ICT training to enable civil servants to work effectively with modern systems and processes, including e-applications such as e-Procurement, e-Budgeting, and e-Information

D. *Education financing products*
- Encourage private-sector-driven financing (scholarships, competitive funds, long-term education loans with income-contingent repayment schemes, and so forth)
- Support the public with subsidies, grants, and targeted education vouchers

BANK INNOVATION SUPPORT AND SCIENCE AND TECHNOLOGY PROJECTS (1980–2003)

Fiscal Year	Country	Project Information	Project Components	Status	Outcomes
1979	Korea	**Electronics Technology Project** Project ID: P004084 TM: Loan amount: US$29 million **Development Objective:** The objectives of the project were to finance the establishment of a research institute in electronics to be called the Korean Institute of Electronics Technology (KIET), to spearhead the Korean electronic industry into advanced semiconductors.	▪ To provide technological infrastructure of essential production and support services for semiconductors; ▪ Assist in training of technical staff of the industry; ▪ Lead the industry in acquiring and developing technologies; ▪ Carry out R&D for industry; and ▪ Explore market opportunities for the industry abroad.	Closed June 1986; 4 years after expected closing date	The loan was made to the Republic of Korea for a project carried out by KIET, which later merged into another institute called Electronics and Telecommunications Research Institute (ETRI). KIET's pioneering efforts in 1979–81 in the acquisition and development of semiconductor technologies and the demonstration effect it had in Korea, and the training provided by KIET to personnel from private entry played an important role in the establishment of this industry. Until 1982 the rapidly growing electronics industry in Korea practically ignored semiconductors. The shift occurred as a result of worldwide shortages in semiconductors, which increased the prices of semiconductors and also severely impaired production of consumer goods. It was then that the leading companies in Korea decided to vertically integrate and move aggressively into semiconductors as well. Accumulated fixed investments in semiconductors in Korea from 1974 to 1981 amounted to about US$200 million. In 1983 alone, investment totaled US$300 million, then climbed to over US$400 million each year for 1984, 1985 and 1986. As a result, Korean firms managed to achieve a prominent position among the world manufacturers. Once the private sector made the decision to go into semiconductors, it did so in a way which dwarfed KIET and, as a result KIET's services became increasingly less attractive. In a broad context, taking into consideration the Korean semiconductor industry's big move in terms of investment in 1983/84 and the huge quantum leap in terms of technological level from 1980/81 to 1983/84, it could be said that the project and KIET may have played an important catalytic role (not a leadership role)

to prove to Korean industry in 1981/82 that Korea, through KIET, in the development of the semiconductors industry in Korea as was originally envisaged.

1989	Hungary	**Third Industrial Restructuring Project** Project ID: P008475 TM: Hiran Heart; Hennie van Greuning Loan amount: US$140 million **Development Objective:** To support the restructuring of the industrial sector to enhance its international competitiveness	▪ Redirecting the product/market mix of the sector to competitive areas suitable for convertible currency exports ▪ Improving enterprise management practices and capabilities ▪ Stimulating the establishment and growth of small business firms, including in the private sector ▪ Alleviating the adverse employment impact of industrial restructuring ▪ Strengthening institutional capabilities in support of industrial restructuring	Closed June 1997

Since lending to Hungary began in 1983, the Bank has focused on supporting the country's program of structural adjustment aimed at making the economy more efficient, flexible, market responsive, and competitive overseas. The Bank was heavily involved in the enterprise sector, providing assistance in formulating a medium-term sector strategy and providing support through nine lending operations. These include four lending operations that are relevant to this loan: the First and Second Industrial Restructuring Projects, which closed in June and September 1993, respectively; the Industrial Sector Adjustment Loan (ISAL), which closed in June 1991; and the Enterprise Reform Loan (ERL), which closed in June 1992. Three restructuring loans in the space of three years, amounting to US$390 million, put a lot of pressure on the counterparts as well as on the financial institutions. The main objectives of this project were conceived for a different economic and business environment, and when this environment changed most of the objectives became obsolete or impossible to achieve. The Bank, in consultation with the Hungarian authorities, consequently amended the loan to better suit the prevailing business environment. The major features of the changes made included: (a) relaxation of the eligibility criteria for investment, such as deletion of the requirement for an export orientation; (b) consolidation of all credit line components under one credit line; (c) opening of the credit line to all sectors; (d) financing of free-standing working

(continued)

Fiscal Year	Country	Project Information	Project Components	Status	Outcomes
					capital; and (e) an increase in the size limit of loans to SMEs from US$150,000 to US$300,000. These changes enabled 985 subloans to be made to SMEs for business development, working capital, and investment financing. With a few exceptions, most banks did not vigorously promote the availability of the Bank credit line, but the collection ratios of the banks nonetheless were around 87 percent. The employment services and retraining component was by far the most successful component of the project.
1990	India	**Industrial Technology Project** Project ID: P009895 TM: Melvin Goldman; Sanjay Kathuria Loan amount: US$200 million **Development Objective:** To facilitate the acquisition and development of technology by industrial firms; to balance domestic technological capability with imported foreign technology; to reduce the financial constraints on new technology ventures; and to reduce foreign exchange constraints on the importation of technology	▪ Helping small, innovative firms obtain financing by supporting the development of venture capital (VC) ▪ Upgrading research and standards institutions to provide technology services to industry, and promoting collaboration between industry and research institutions ▪ Financing the importation of technology and technical knowhow by industry by supporting the fast-track Technology Development Fund (TDF)	Closed 1997, two years after scheduled closing date	The project was able to bolster the speed at which reforms moved toward liberalization, and a large part of the original funding was in the end not required. Four hundred firms benefited from this financing to upgrade their technological capabilities. The project additionally supported six venture capital companies (VCCs), which managed nine funds. The VCCs invested in more than 300 companies, with returns averaging around 18–20 percent. Because of the lack of other sources of technology finance, many of these ventures would not have been possible without the intervention of the VCCs. (The project in fact effectively launched the VC industry in India, and indirectly influenced the culture of risk finance.) The project supported 33 loans in 30 Technology Institutions, providing loans rather than grants to oblige the TIs to focus on financial management and rates of return. Many research institutes additionally were able to modernize their physical facilities, enabling them to reorient themselves to serve industry. Most of these institutions have significantly raised the proportion of the budget that comes from their own earnings. The Spon-

sored R&D (SPREAD) promotion fund component of the project similarly showed strong positive results. Many borrowers had never undertaken any R&D activity before and had no previous activities with a TI. Most companies borrowing under SPREAD were small or of medium size, but many of the technologies developed were complex, involved substantial technological effort, and introduced completely new products or processes to India. Exports often resulted from SPREAD projects.

1991	Republic of Korea	**Universities Science and Technology Project** Project ID: P004129 TM: n/a Loan amount: US$45 million **Development Objective:** To assist selected universities in broadening and deepening their basic research programs in priority fields in science and technology; and to improve the training of science teachers through the enhancement of research capacity in this field which in turn will strengthen the base of science education in the secondary schools.	Supporting the financing of specialized research equipment, consumable materials, and equipment-related operation and O&M expenditures to strengthen: ■ research programs in graduate schools of natural science, and engineering in selected public and private universities ■ joint research facilities in selected universities, to promote the cost-effective utilization of advanced research equipment ■ selected university departments of science education, to improve research in areas of pedagogy and science subjects	Closed 1995	The project successfully met its objectives, as evidenced by: (a) the utilization of more than 3,150 items of research equipment supplied by the project; (b) the large number of completed research projects (1,132) and a publication rate of the research results of 91 percent; (c) an increase in registered patent rights in the project institutions; and (d) a significant expansion of practical instruction in science education departments. Research capacity was increased during the term of the project: a total of 1,621 research projects were selected, of which 70 percent were completed, 27 percent are ongoing, and the remaining 3 percent are in the initiation stage. The latter projects lagged due to the delayed delivery of some research equipment. The findings of 117 research projects, 67 conducted by public universities and 50 by private universities, were adopted by private firms. The project design was consistent with sectoral objectives and the broader goals of technology-intensive industrialization in Korea. The project was based on more than a decade of previous Bank support for technology development in Korea that had focused on financing R&D projects through financial intermediaries, strengthening those intermediaries,

(continued)

Fiscal Year	Country	Project Information	Project Components	Status	Outcomes
					enhancing the R&D capacity of the national research institutes, and developing technical and scientific education. At the time of preparation the Bank had financed projects in electronics technology and industry promotion; it also had started to assist R&D activities in the universities under Loan 2427-KO and in the national research institutes under the first Technology Advancement Project (Loan 3037-KO). The project was designed within a sound policy environment, developed with considerable assistance from the Bank's two education sector loans (Loan 1800-KO and Loan 2427-KO) that had addressed policy issues in research and in science and technology education. The project continued the assistance to graduate programs, basic research in science and technology, and the strengthening of science education that the Bank had begun with Loan 2427-KO.
1991	Algeria	**Science and Technology University Development Project** Project ID: P004934 TM: Mourad Ezzine Loan amount: US$65 million **Development Objective:** To provide an institutional model (based on peer review and transparency) for the allocation of investment resources to higher	▪ Improving university management and administration ▪ Improving curriculum relevance, teaching quality, and teacher qualifications in selected S&T degree programs that target specific needs of the labor market ▪ Improving the contribution of the universities to regional and national development through the forging of closer research and training links with local industry	Closed June 1998, two years after the scheduled closing date	The project did not achieve all of its objectives. However, its implementation had a positive impact on the teaching and research capacities and on the management of the selected universities. The Science and Technology University Development Project was the first Bank project in the higher education sector. It was initiated in 1988 and developed as a pilot experience aimed at increasing university autonomy and efficiency in the context of a scarcity of resources, the result of the sharp drop in country oil revenues that began in 1986. Conception and implementation of the project coincided with a dramatic degradation of the political and security situation in Algeria. Throughout the 10-year period of the project its implementation was severely constrained by the unfavorable environment, but

	education and to assist the Government in upgrading undergraduate and post-graduate teaching and research, concentrating on the three major universities of science and technology.			it did realize some improvements in the quality of teaching and research, as evidenced by the following indicators: (a) an increase in the number of postgraduate diplomas; (b) a reduction in the duration of studies for completion of doctorates; (c) a reduction in the numbers of repeater students; (d) an increase in the use of libraries and documentation centers; (e) an increase in the number of scientific publications of international standard; and (f) an increase in the use of laboratories. The full potential of the project to improve teaching and research conditions was not realized due in large part to the difficulties encountered by Algerians in obtaining visas to travel abroad and to the reluctance of foreign nationals to go to Algeria. The project was successful in providing universities with needed scientific and pedagogical equipment.
1991	**Rural Industrial Technology (Spark) Project** Project ID: P003529 TM: Helen Chan Loan amount: US$114.3 million **Development Objective:** To provide institutional support services to rural enterprises through the provision to the national Spark program of training, technical and management information, technical evaluation	China	▪ Providing credit to those town and village enterprises (TVEs) that are implementing approved Spark subprojects to introduce new or upgraded production technology and/or product design ▪ Supporting programs to upgrade the skills of rural enterprise managers and workers, by providing technical assistance and training to Spark training managers and instructors. Helping Institute of Scientific and Technical Information of China adapt its information network to reach TVEs with business-oriented information by (a) providing technical assistance, (b) providing training and	Closed 1997	Project results were mixed. The technical assistance components were highly satisfactory, but the results of the enterprise modernization component were unsatisfactory. The technical assistance components were pleasing for several reasons: (a) the government completed all technical assistance components with great efficiency; (b) these activities provided essential support to the TVE sector, which had exhibited extraordinary growth in the previous decade; and (c) the national Spark program was strengthened as a result. However, most sub-borrowers of the enterprise modernization component did not repay their loans, with the result that the Participating Financial Institutions and ultimately the provincial/municipal finance bureaus would have to bear the financial cost. Overall, with the support of local Science and Technology Bureau, many of the Spark subprojects became pillar industries of

(continued)

Fiscal Year	Country	Project Information	Project Components	Status	Outcomes
		methodology, and consultant services; and to provide financial support to the ongoing Spark program	equipment for the development of new databases, (c) improving electronic and other information systems, and (d) upgrading delivery networks in the project areas ■ Developing institutions by strengthening implementation capabilities within the State Science and Technology Commission		their respective "Spark-intensive" areas, providing not only direct and indirect employment opportunities but also increasing the vertical and horizontal integration of local industries. The Chongming Training Center, despite its geographic disadvantage, has evolved into a high-quality intensive training center in the Shanghai area, and its utilization rate has been 100 percent for more than two years.
1991	Hungary	**Human Resources Development Project** Project ID: P008483 TM: Gyorgy Novotny Loan amount: US$150 million **Development Objective:** To address human resources issues that are preventing successful transition to a market economy	■ Assisting unemployed workers to find jobs, and enterprises to find suitable workers ■ Providing relevant training for youth and adults ■ Improving the responsiveness of higher education to the new technical and managerial demands of a market economy; ■ Narrowing the technological gap by expanding and reorienting the training of science and technology researchers, improving management of research and improving the linkages between academic community and enterprises; ■ Developing foreign language competency	Closed June 1997, one year after the scheduled closing date	Since lending to Hungary began in 1983, the Bank has focused on supporting the country's program of structural adjustment aimed at making the economy more efficient, flexible, market responsive, and competitive overseas. In the first eight years the Bank was heavily involved in industrial, agricultural, and infrastructure restructuring. The Human Resources Development Project (HRDP) was the first loan to give assistance across a broad spectrum of human resources issues, including labor markets, training, higher education, and science and technology research. The project successfully met all of its objectives. It equipped the employment network, adult and youth training centers, higher educational institutes, and research centers with state-of-the-art facilities and training equipment. A modern labor statistics system was developed; a short-term (six-month) labor forecast model was adopted; public employment services were modernized; eight new Regional Labor Development Training Centers (RLDCs) and 31 new mobile centers were established, covering the entire country and providing training to about 10,000 persons per annum; new education systems, including

				the development of new curricula and vocational training, were introduced in 79 vocational secondary schools; through a competition-based funding system the higher education and the connecting basic research activity were modernized, better equipped, and became capable of providing training and services on a Western European level; universities were empowered to award research degrees; three-year retraining courses were organized for more than 2,000 language teachers; and new language training methodology and communication-oriented curricula were introduced.
1991	Brazil	**Science Research and Training (PADCT II) Project** Project ID: P006483 TM: Alcyone Saliba Loan amount: US$150 million **Development Objective:** to strengthen human resource development in specific science areas through support for science research and graduate training.	▓ Providing competitive grants for research and training in six scientific areas (biotechnology, chemistry and chemical engineering, geo-sciences and mineral technology, instrumentation, new materials and environmental sciences); and in six support areas (primary and secondary science education, science planning and management, basic industrial technology, science technology information, provision of consumable, and maintenance of scientific equipment). ▓ Enhancing human resources development by (a) financing short courses; (b) using foreign consultants; (c) providing overseas training for professionals; (d) establishing exchanges of foreign researchers; and (e) supporting professionals in specific research projects	Closed 1996, one year after the scheduled closing date	The goal of PADCT II was to continue to improve the management and decision-making processes that were established under the PADCT I. Its methodology was to use open competition for research grants, interaction between government agencies and the scientific community, and greater continuity and integration in the financing of research projects. A total of 1,809 projects, implemented by more than 350 institutions, were approved for assistance. The average project size (US$168,000) was significantly higher than under PADCT I (US$70,000), thus achieving a decrease in the scattering of resources. In all, 78 percent of projects and 80 percent of resources went to projects in institutions from the southern and southeastern states of Brazil. Many basic research projects resulted in the creation of new technologies, processes, and products. However, only a few of the sampled projects in the five "mainstream" research areas (biotechnology, geosciences, chemistry, new materials, and instrumentation) found their way into industrial applications. About one-third of projects developed products and 18 percent applied

(continued)

Fiscal Year	Country	Project Information	Project Components	Status	Outcomes
					for patents, but fewer than 5 percent of projects developed products that were commercialized and only 6 percent resulted in technology transfers. PADCT II nonetheless contributed to a strengthening of Brazil's basic technological infrastructure. In particular, it has helped to overcome serious gaps in the infrastructure of the National Metrology Laboratory system. Through the Quality Management Program (PEGQ) it also promoted the voluntary application of quality control management in industry, training 24,000 professionals from public and private organizations and contributing to the large increase in enterprises certified to ISO 9000 standards from 18 in 1991 to more than 2,000 by mid-1997. Finally, an important organizational change in the Brazilian S&T system occurred on 9 January 1996, with the creation of the interministerial National Council for Science and Technology (CCT). The CCT serves as a superior advisory body to the President, with a broad legal mandate to propose national S&T policy.
1992	Turkey	**Technology Development Project** Project ID: P009058 TM: Vinod K. Goel Loan amount: US$100 million **Development Objective:** To develop the MSTQ (metrology, standards, testing, and quality) system to	▣ Upgrading MSTQ through development of a National Metrology Institute, improvements in the Turkish Standards Institute, and setting up a National Accreditation Council (that in turn would set up the Professional Institute for Quality Assurance) ▣ Establishing funds to stimulate the amount of applied R&D conducted by industry, in a mix of matching grants, income notes and conditional loans,	Closed December 1998, 18 months after scheduled closing date	The project resulted in the setting up of the National Metrology Institute (UME), which has 25 laboratories. UME performs calibration services and conducts some R&D. The Turkish Standards Institute (TSE) was strengthened through the setting up of a modern Quality Campus in Istanbul. Modern financial and management information systems have been established that have streamlined the cost accounting, budgeting, and management reporting functions in TSE, but an independent National Accreditation Council (NAC) was not established until the follow-up project that currently is under supervision. The Technology

	Project	Objectives	Status	Results
		international standards; to encourage market-oriented R&D in the private sector by financing projects on a matching basis; and to foster the growth of a venture capital (VC) industry • and seed capital for studies on the competitiveness of strategic industries • Facilitating the growth of the VC industry by defining a legal and regulatory structure for VC and providing appropriate tax treatment for VC funds; and by establishing a VC company and fund to act as a role model for the industry		Development Foundation of Turkey (TTGV) was established and supported 103 R&D projects and sector/foresight studies. Private sector participation in technology development projects was in excess of 50 percent, and a large majority of projects have been technically and commercially successful. Overall, TTGV has been successful in initiating a culture of R&D and technology finance in Turkey. The project additionally helped the legal and regulatory framework in Turkey to become more conducive to the growth of venture capital, and the follow-on operation currently under supervision has seen TTGV take an equity stake in two venture capital companies.
1992	**Engineering and Science Education Project** Project ID: P004591 TM: Ompom Regel Loan amount: US$85 million **Development Objective:** To upgrade industrial and technological capability by increasing the supply of high-level S&T manpower	• Improving the institutional framework of engineering and science education; strengthening financial and resource management; matching enrollments to S&T manpower needs; and improving accreditation • Offering support and services to ensure the provision of biotechnology consumables; implanting a system of online electronic dissemination; and establishing a system of monitoring and evaluation • Implementing an investment program to finance qualitative improvements in engineering education, science education and research, technology management, library networks, secondary school science and mathematics, and S&T manpower planning	Closed June 1998, one year after the scheduled closing date	The Bank has been involved since 1965 in the education sector in the Philippines, operating 14 education and training projects for a total financing of US$767.5 million. This latest program enhanced the quality and relevance of engineering and science education through faculty and program upgrading, investment in facilities and equipment, and improved linkages with industry. Science laboratories at 110 secondary schools have been upgraded and equipped, curricula revised, and more than 1,000 teachers trained. Local capacities for science and mathematics teacher training have been strengthened by the upgrading of science laboratories at 22 teacher training institutions and through the improvement of the teacher trainer qualifications. Undergraduate enrollments at the 19 intermediate engineering colleges in the priority fields targeted increased from 19,267 in 1990/91 (baseline) to 21,600 in 1997/98 (project completion), an increase of 12 percent. MS/PhD enrollments almost doubled from 200 to 380 over the same period, or almost 2 percent of undergraduate enrollment, as planned. As regards

(continued)

Fiscal Year	Country	Project Information	Project Components	Status	Outcomes
					quality improvements, an aggressive faculty development program (PhD and MS/MEng), covering about 800 faculties, was completed in 2000 with government financing. Laboratories at 19 engineering schools were upgraded. Thirteen network schools established formal linkages with industry, and graduate programs and short-term courses in the management of technology were introduced as options at three flagship institutions (Asian Institute of Management, De La Salle University, and University of the Philippines-Diliman). Libraries at seven science and three engineering colleges were improved as planned.
1992	Kenya	**Universities Investment Project** Project ID: P001362 TM: Bruce Jones Loan amount: US$55 million **Development Objective:** To support the government's education sector adjustment program through provision of an investment-oriented complement to the Education Sector Adjustment Credit (EdSAC)	■ Rationalizing and strengthening the institutional framework for higher education in the public and private sectors ■ Limiting growth of the borrowed budgetary resources devoted to the public universities by promoting cost sharing and improved investment planning ■ Improving the quality of teaching and research at public universities	Closed 1999, 2.5 years after the scheduled closing date	About 600 university staff were trained, mainly at the master's degree, diploma, and certificate levels. Eight Applied Research projects shared the funds that had been allocated for this purpose, with five already generating reasonable income. The Higher Education Loans Board (HELB) advises that the percentage of loanees with mature loans who are repaying has increased from 10 percent in 1995 to 38 percent in June 1999. The universities calculate the unit costs of various degree programs and place more emphasis on raising their own revenues, including by enrolling "parallel" students who are not sponsored by the government. The seven Primary Teacher Training Colleges initiated under the Sixth Education Project, and also receiving funds from the Universities Investment Credit, account for about 30 percent of the total teacher training capacity in government institutions in Kenya. The six of these colleges that are operating have helped to enable the replacement of untrained teachers, such that there are no longer any untrained teachers employed.

| 1993 | Republic of Korea | **Science Education and Libraries Computerization Project**

Project ID: P004165

TM: Robert McGough

Loan amount: US$50 million

Development Objective: To assist in improving the quality of basic science education and to create effective links between the university libraries that service teaching and research | ▓ Raising the quality of science programs offered in secondary-level science education centers and in undergraduate basic science programs in selected universities, to strengthen the quality of science and engineering degrees

▓ Establishing a computerized, interlibrary network linking 37 institutions, to enhance the access to information of students, faculty, and researchers | Closed 1997 | The science education centers of the secondary schools and the joint science centers of the national universities have raised the quality of science education and increased its relevance given the rapidly changing technology of the workplace. Secondary school graduates have been able to find employment or have continued to universities and colleges. The computerized library network, linking all public and private university libraries, is in full operation at its planned scale. The use of a new operating system was a key factor behind the increase in the number of research programs and scientific publications that emerged during the project years. |
| 1993 | Mexico | **Science and Technology Infrastructure (PACIME) Project**

Project ID: P007676

TM: Daniel Crisafulli

Loan amount: US$189 million

Development Objective: To improve the competitiveness of domestic firms and attract foreign investment; to | ▓ Supporting increased public spending, (a) for grants for basic scientific research projects and equipment infrastructure projects, with improved allocation on a competitive basis; and (b) for technology infrastructure in the area of MSTQ and intellectual property protection, to improve services to industry, to enhance competitiveness, and to increase attractiveness for foreign investment

▓ Developing institutions, through support for the restructuring of the science research program, that in turn | Closed 1998 | The project met its objectives, as evidenced by an increase in the number of scientific research publications and their impact, the production of a significant number of personnel trained in research, a renewal of the Mexican research instrumentation infrastructure, the institutionalization of merit-based peer review, and improvements in the efficiency of the National Science and Technology Council. The creation of the Mexican National Center for Metrology is helping to attract foreign investment and is promoting the competitiveness of Mexican industry. In tandem with the creation of a this metrology capability, policies to stimulate private sector demand for services and for the formation of a secondary, private metrology network will be critical to the achievement of a significant medium-term |

(continued)

Fiscal Year	Country	Project Information	Project Components	Status	Outcomes
		embark on a program of long-term institutional development	provide support to industry in terms of MSTQ and intellectual property protection		impact on the competitiveness of local industry. The project supported the creation of the Mexican Institute of Industrial Property, significantly reducing delays in the award of patents, increasing enforcement activities, and increasing inspections related to intellectual property violations. Institutional strengthening and the creation of an internationally respected Intellectual Property Rights agency should enable the development of a systemic approach to address weaknesses in the judicial system and broader issues in the creation, diffusion, and application of technical knowledge in the country. Although support for the creation of basic S&T infrastructure was deemed appropriate given the chronic under-investment of the 1980s, however, the project should have incorporated measures to promote articulation of demand for S&T services and for a linkage of research to societal needs. A second weakness of project design was of its failure to introduce incentives to link research with teaching, thus potentially reducing the impact of research on the formation of skilled human resources.
1993	Tunisia	**Higher Education Restructuring Project** Project ID: P005726 TM: Francis Steier, Jeffrey Waite Loan amount: US$75 million **Development Objective:** To make the higher education system	▪ Diversifying the higher education system through the creation of higher institutes of technology, to improve the creation of a trained technical and managerial labor force ▪ Providing incentives to encourage universities to reexamine and review their curricula, with a view to strengthening the quality of education and academic attainment	Closed 2001, three years after the scheduled closing date	The creation of a new generation of institutions of higher education (ISETs) has diversified Tunisian higher education, such that it now is developing middle-level technicians and managers for the labor force. The nature of the ISETs (training of senior technicians, ties to the economic environment, status of specialist teaching staff, greater autonomy in institutional management) has not only made them more responsive to the country's economic needs but has also served as a model for an in-depth reform of the entire higher education system. As a direct outcome of the competi-

					Status
		more responsive to the country's needs; and to improve its performance in economic terms (cost effectiveness) and human terms (proportion of university entrants who graduate)	■ Improving resource distribution and use according to set strategies, by creating a new normative system of budgetary allocation and through the development of a new management system adapted to the needs of more autonomous institutions of higher education	tive fund for innovation (PNRU) activities and the indirect example of the ISETs, most universities have now reviewed their curricula with a view to strengthening the quality of education and academic attainment. In addition, the Ministry of Higher Education is now fully involved in the accreditation of all new university programs. However, although all PNRU projects met the criteria set out, fully one-third of the projects were submitted by the MHE itself, and not by universities, as was planned. It is clear that a culture of promoting performance through competition for additional resources has not yet been developed. Resource distribution and use appear to have improved, although it remains unclear whether or not this improvement can be attributed solely to the project. Finally, the higher education management information system (SAGES) of the MHE appears key to the rationalization process and its managerial training has had considerable impact.	
1994	Mali	**National Agricultural Research Project** Project ID: P001751 TM: Marie-Helene Collion, Agadiou Dama Loan amount: US$20 Million **Development Objective:** To ensure that adequate technology will become available to farmers as a means to increase agricultural growth	■ Improving institutional capacity of the National Agricultural Research Council and National Agricultural Research Institute IER ■ Supporting Technology Transfer and User Participation through improving interactions between researchers, farmers and extension staff; establishing of a pilot research fund available to contract for research. ■ Improving research quality and relevance through improved research programming, monitoring and evaluation methods and procedures; strengthening	The project achieved its objective of improving the performance of the national agricultural research system. The project achieved fundamental changes in the structure and management of research, increased user participation and external reviews of the quality of ongoing and proposed research activities. There were, however, some serious delays in project implementation that negatively impacted on the strengthening of human resource management, financial management and monitoring and evaluation remain weak. Collaboration between research and its natural partners (extension, producer organizations, NGOs) was strengthened through the creation of research user committees, regular regional technical review meetings, and the	Closed 2001

(continued)

Fiscal Year	Country	Project Information	Project Components	Status	Outcomes
		and to reverse the decline in the productive capacity of the natural resource base.	external linkages and supporting the participation of Malian institutions and scientists in regional and international collaborative research programs. ■ Improving resource development and management, rehabilitating and renewing research experiment station and equipment.		establishment of a research fund managed by the research user committees which permitted these to contract out research activities with IER that were a priority to them. Regional collaboration was substantially strengthened through the project. Twelve out of the sixteen research programs are now executed in collaboration with regional and international agricultural research organizations in adapting promising technologies to local circumstances. A total of 120 new technologies were introduced by IER, of which 110 were disseminated by the extension services and were adopted to different degrees by farmers. The technologies were mainly focused on reducing the risks from climatic change, improving production (rice, fruits and vegetables, and poultry) and quality of crops intended for transformation (cotton, corn, honey). Adoption rates were closely linked to potential income increases, input requirements (labor and non-labor inputs) and availability, access to credit, and risk of crop failure.
1994	Malaysia	**Polytechnic Development Project** Project ID: P004309 TM: Omporn Regel Loan amount: US$107 million **Development Objective:** To improve the efficiency and capacity of technical education through establish-	■ Establishing three new polytechnics at Shah Alam, Penang (at Seberang Prai), and Johor Bahru to create about 13,000 additional training places ■ Reforming policy and strengthening institutions by: (a) supporting a training system driven by employer demand; (b) introducing cost recovery and operational efficiency; (c) decentralizing the control of polytechnic institutes; and (d) improving capacity utiliza-	Closed 1999	The following achievements were recorded at project completion: (a) a more decentralized, demand-driven polytechnic system was put in place; (b) a National Advisory Committee was established for the system; (c) local-level industry/education advisory committees were established in all polytechnics; (d) cost recovery policies were introduced, including time share programs with firms in existing institutions, a 25 percent increase in employer-sponsored training, and the establishment of a student fee of 2,000 ringgit (about US$525 at US$1 = RM3.8) per semester; (e) facility optimization policies were initiated for all institu-

		lishing training practices that are market-oriented; and to reduce structural unemployment and encourage greater labor absorption and mobility	▪ Establishing a Polytechnic Staff Training Center to train teachers, including the recruitment and training of about 1,000 new teachers and instructors or project institutions ▪ Upgrading curricula and developing new courses to expand the services offered by the polytechnic system ▪ Carrying out three studies for the improvement of the polytechnic system ▪ Training to strengthen the Human Resources Development Fund (HRDF) ▪ Training to strengthen the National Vocational Training Council		tions; and (f) career guidance counselors were introduced to reduce drop-out rates. The staff development component successfully trained (a) 579 students in a Master's (Technical Education) program, many of whom are serving as polytechnic lecturers (and a further 121 students in 2000); (b) 740 students in B.Sc. Engineering, exceeding the target of 600; and (c) 193 students in diploma courses, compared with the target of 200. 110 scholarships were awarded for bachelor degree courses in local universities, with 100 students completing their training. Curriculum development was achieved through two training courses conducted for 22 participants from all 12 polytechnics. The system is now being institutionalized in all polytechnics. The HRDF component that sought to encourage private sector firms to provide company-specific training programs saw the successful implementation of local and overseas training activities, with most completed during the first year of project implementation. Three HRDC staff completed short-term training in Taiwan, the United States, and Australia.
1994	Republic of Korea	**Science and Technical Education Project** Project ID: P004168 TM: Carol Hau-Lai Ball Loan amount: US$190 million **Development Objective:** To assist in improving the quality of science and technical	▪ Supporting quality improvements in undergraduate science and engineering departments in selected universities ▪ Strengthening the teaching and research capacity of marine science institutions ▪ Helping improve the quality of practical science and engineering programs in the open universities (OUs) and in selected junior technical colleges (JTCs) ▪ Improving opportunities for junior research activities in basic sciences by strengthening	Closed 1999	Under the guidance of the MOE, the project facilitated and enhanced research capabilities and teaching programs at 36 university engineering departments, 41 university natural science departments, 10 marine science institutions, nine OUs, eight JTCs, and 19 VHSs. The research outputs were impressive. The number of research projects more than doubled from 4,105 in 1995 to more than 10,000 in 1999. A total of 40,929 research activities were conducted during the implementation period (about 50 percent more than appraisal estimates). The results of 87 percent of these activities were published domestically or internationally, 12 percent were used by

(continued)

Fiscal Year	Country	Project Information	Project Components	Status	Outcomes
		education and research through implementation of a Ministry of Education (MOE) policies and actions program	facilities at the Korea Basic Science Institute (KBSI) (formerly the Korea Basic Science Center) ■ Enhancing the quality of training in vocational high schools (VHSs)		related industries, and 2 percent were awarded patents. More than 40,000 joint research projects were conducted with universities, research institutes, and industrial companies during the implementation period, approximately 600 of which were published domestically and internationally. The project further benefited the project institutions and other institutions, including several in the private sector, through making available to them the procured equipment. For example, nine major national universities in Korea allocated 29.4 percent of their loan allocations to their research and teaching support institutes, which provide common facilities and equipment to users from inside and outside the project universities. Similarly, equipment provided to the Korea Marine University was utilized for training by private organizations and industry.
1994	Kenya	**Micro and Small Enterprise Training and Technology Project** Project ID: P001353 TM: Ivan Rossignol Loan Amount: US$ 21.83 Million **Development Objective:** To enhance the entrepreneurial development in the private sector and, more specifically, reduce constraints to employment pro-	■ Establishing a micro- and small enterprise training fund to provide incentives for skill upgrading and technology development. ■ Supporting Technology Information/Innovation and Research Program to stimulate information exchange and innovation in product development. ■ Designing a small pilot program of adaptive technology research grants to promote the indigenous capacity for the research, design, and commercialization of new products and production technologies for the informal sector.	Closed 2002, one year after the scheduled closing date	Entrepreneurial development in the private sector was enhanced and constraints to employment promotion and income enhancement in the micro- and small-enterprise (informal) sector were reduced. A total of 34,778 micro-enterprise owners and workers received training in four years out of a total of 172,000 micro-enterprise units estimated in the 1999 census. Of these, 70% were trained in technical areas and 30% in management. 60% of all trainees were women, greatly exceeding the target of 20%. The provision of training at the nationwide level has greatly exceeded the target of 24,000 revised in 1998 and also surpassed the target of 32,000 set in 1997. 80% of trainees reported growth in their business (as against 13% in the control group), and 61% had added business assets (vs. 21%);

		motion and income enhancement in the micro- and small-enterprise (informal) sector.	▪ Developing a new partnership between the public and private sector guaranteeing the full participation for Jua Kali entrepreneurs and workers in training and technology policy and program decisions and subsequent implementation.	Under technology development components, 1275 voucher clients and 79 Savings and Credit Cooperatives officials were trained, three sectoral exhibitions were held, and 12 sub-sectoral studies were carried out. The project played a major role in enhancing information exchange and business networks among MSEs.
1995	Indonesia	**University Research for Graduate Education Project** Project ID: P004017 TM: Halsey L. Beemer, Jr. Loan amount: US$58.9 million **Development Objective:** To improve the quality of graduate education, attract more qualified candidates for domestic graduate education, and strengthen research capacity and dissemination of research findings in universities.	▪ Improving planning and management for graduate education and university research by providing assistance to the University Research Council (URC) ▪ Supporting competitive grant and fellowship programs to strengthen the incentives for institutions, university staff, and graduate students to participate in high-quality graduate training and research activities (the grant program supported the following: (a) the center grant program; (b) research grant programs; (c) graduate education programs; (d) scientific publication programs; (e) domestic collaborative research grants; and (f) international research linkages)	Closed 2001, one year after the scheduled closing date The Center Grant Program, which focused on the creation of scientific research units led by younger Indonesian academics, provided a dynamic environment within which young graduate students and researchers were able to carry on their work in Indonesia rather than going abroad. The program to prepare junior faculty from second- and third-tier institutions for graduate education helped them compete more successfully for access to programs at first-tier institutions. As these junior faculty members returned to their home universities, it became apparent that this approach to raising the academic quality of the home institutions worked better than previous systems that sought to encourage graduates of first-tier institutions to move down the scale. In addition, funding made available to researchers from outside-project-supported research units to carry out collaborative research with project-supported researchers expanded the impact of projects well beyond their original institution focus. The provision of these network-supporting funds by the Domestic Collaborative Research Grants program enabled greater use by researchers countrywide of project-developed resources and research programs. The Graduate Team Research Program and the Young Academic Program were also able to increase the research capacity of the graduate supervisors, and this in turn benefited graduate students and graduate

(continued)

Fiscal Year	Country	Project Information	Project Components	Status	Outcomes
1995	Mauritius	**Technical Assistance to Enhance Competitiveness Project** Project ID: P001918 TL: Ahmet Soylemezoglu Loan amount: US$6.7 million **Development Objective:** To help firms enhance their competitiveness and thereby improve the prospects for sustainable rapid growth. To be achieved by facilitating private sector access to know-how to help improve productivity, quality, design, and response times, and to diversify export production	■ Supporting a Technology Diffusion Scheme (TDS) to help firms access specialized technical and marketing know-how ■ Creating the basic institutional infrastructure for MSTQ-related services, and creating a national quality system ■ Supporting an Electronic Trade Facilitation System (ETFS) ■ Providing technical assistance in (a) the development of productivity and competitiveness indicators and improvement of the monitoring of industrial development; (b) review of the Retirement Savings System; and (c) the restructuring of the Investment Authorization System	Closed 1999	education programs. The focus on strengthening domestic institutions rather than sending researchers abroad created a stronger and potentially more sustainable domestic human capacity training. The TDS project realized its overall objective of helping firms gain access to specialized technical and marketing know-how. This was achieved through a significant transfer of technical resources to private enterprises, achieved by means of a grant instrument that financed the technology transfer on a cost-sharing basis. The TDS helped 190 firms implement 266 different projects. Another key project target was enhanced export performance. Although the project did not set specific export targets for participant firms, the export performance of these firms surpassed industry averages and the national export growth rate: exports by participant firms rose 53 percent compared to an overall export increase of 21 percent in 1996 and 3 percent in 1997. Exports by participant firms in the export processing zone (EPZ) grew about 61 percent, compared to growth rates of 15 percent in 1996 and 10 percent in 1997 achieved across all EPZ firms. There additionally was a marked increase in the range of products that are exported. Alongside the TDS, the government set up a similar matching grant fund with its own resources, to be administered by the Ministry of Industry and Commerce. Efforts to strengthen the Mauritius Standards Bureau (MSB) have afforded the bureau international credibility, enabling it to join the International Standards Organization (ISO) and enabling Mauritius to meet WTO requirements. The Electronic Trade Facilitation System (ETFS) component of the project

reduced the processing time of trade documentation from about two–four days to 15 minutes, with 24-hour availability. All users of the system, including customs officials, were trained in the new system. The ETFS infrastructure will also provide services for the Mauritius Offshore Business Activities Authority, making it a sustained initiative.

| 1995 | Ghana | **Private Sector Development Project** Project ID: P000960 TM: Kofi Boateng-Agyen, Michael Wong Loan amount: US$13 million **Development Objective:** To increase and deepen the private sector contribution to economic growth, and in particular to improve private sector competitiveness in global markets | ■ Providing training and technical assistance to the Secretariat of the Council for Scientific and Industrial Research (CSIR) and four institutions to develop a commercialization strategy to serve the needs of the private sector, and assisting the Ghana Standards Board (GSB) to develop metrology and quality testing standards
■ Forming a Technology and Enterprise Development Fund (TEDF) to assist private SMEs to develop products and provide services, to develop their technical and financial plans to a level of bankable quality and feasibility, and to support their efforts to raise funds or investor support
■ Supporting a study to determine the market demand for the Ghana Trade Fair Authority (GTFA) and an architectural survey to assess the rehabilitation and redesign needs of the GTFA pavilions
■ Supporting a feasibility study to determine the scope, financial viability, commercial demand, | Closed 2000 | The macroeconomic fundamentals of Ghana have been deteriorating since the credit was approved, and it is likely that this resulted in changed perceptions and priorities and affected project outcome. The project helped create a greater consciousness of markets and commercial practices among all participating institutions, which is an important step toward achieving the project objective of restructuring, reforming, and commercializing these institutions. The actual progress of some of the beneficiary institutions in meeting project objectives was limited, but significant progress was made in improving the performance of the GSB and in the modernization of the legal infrastructure, and Bank support for these activities will be continued under another Bank project. The second key project component, the TEDF, had limited impact. Its outcome was adversely affected not only because of its design, but also by the adverse investment climate in the country. |

(continued)

Fiscal Year	Country	Project Information	Project Components	Status	Outcomes
			and organizational structure for the Industrial Design Center ▪ Supporting a study of ways to improve the delivery of legal services and assistance, to strengthen the capacity of government to support the delivery of services		
1995	Brazil	**Science and Technology Subprogram: Project Science Centers and Directed Research Phase I** Project ID: P006568 TM: Judith M. Lisansky Loan amount: US$15.8 million **Development Objective:** To promote the generation and dissemination of scientific knowledge relevant to conservation and sustainable development activities in the Amazon region	▪ Supporting a grants program for the competitive funding of research projects in the Amazon region ▪ Strengthening two established research institutions of the Amazon, the National Institute for Amazon Research (INPA) in Manaus and the Emilio Goeldi Museum of Para (MPEG) in Belem	Closed 1999, two years after the scheduled closing date	Twenty-three research projects were selected in 1995. Directed Research subproject executors included INPA, the Brazilian Agricultural Research Corporation (EMBRAPA), the National Institute for Space Research (INPE), and the Brazilian Cocoa Development Agency (CEPLAC), along with other Amazonian institutions (comprising mainly universities and one NGO). About 26 regional institutions, 17 national agencies from other states, and nine international institutions participated in the implementation of the projects, indicating a strong inter-institutional and interdisciplinary integration. In addition, 51 national and 26 international institutions cooperated with the subproject executing institutions, indicating both a worldwide interest in Amazonian issues and an evident effort toward multi-institutional cooperation. The majority of the subprojects (14) produced results or partial results; most of the projects reporting no results were mainly long-term projects needing further research before reliable conclusions could be drawn. The Directed Research subprojects also contributed to the introduction of innovative methodological techniques for wider use in Amazon research activities. Other main achievements included: (a) the restructuring and prioritization of research programs; (b) the definition of strategic objectives of the

Science Centers; and (c) the introduction of competitive fund allocation systems to support research projects within each institution. The effort to upgrade human resources saw a 34 percent increase in the number of PhDs at INPA and a 54 percent increase at MPEG, and at project completion most of the remaining research staff of both institutes were registered in graduate courses. Participation of the researchers at national and international scientific congresses was significantly expanded, and the postgraduate program for nonstaff researchers that is provided by INPA and MPEG was considerably increased. Infrastructural improvements also were made that were essential to the preservation of the various scientific collections at both centers: both centers furthermore expanded their collections and modernized and computerized their management.

| 1995 | Indonesia | **Second Professional Human Resource Development Project**

Project ID: P003988

TM: Christopher James Smith

Loan amount: US$69 million

Development Objective: To foster economic development and industrialization and to facilitate policies of deregulation and decentralization by upgrading the | ▪ Supporting fellowships and the training components of three elements with a similar range of activities but aimed at different client groups and subject areas (the Overseas Training Office (OTO), Ministry of Finance (MOF), and Science and Technology for Industrial Development (STAID))

▪ Supporting the National Steering Team for Overseas Training (NASTOT) component to help NASTOT play a more effective role in formulating policy; and coordinating and monitoring the civil service fellowships and the pilot programs for fresh graduates | Closed 2001 |

(continued)

Fiscal Year	Country	Project Information	Project Components	Status	Outcomes
		quality of professional, managerial, science, and technology staff in key government ministries and agencies at the local and national levels and, on a limited scale, in the private sector			
1996	Thailand	**Universities Science and Engineering Education Project** Project ID: P004805 TM: William Rees Loan amount: US$143.4 million **Development Objective:** To improve the quality of undergraduate science and engineering programs	▪ Strengthening the teaching capabilities of faculty ▪ Upgrading the content of existing programs in science and engineering and broaden the range of programs relevant to Thailand's technological advancement ▪ Modernizing laboratories and strengthening their management ▪ Improving the utilization of resources in faculties of engineering and science, and establishing a system for the large-scale procurement of equipment ▪ Supporting project management by financing office facilities and equipment; the employment of local consultants, support staff, and temporary staff; and, for project implementation staff, short-term local and overseas training in management techniques	Expected closing date is December 2003	

| 1996 | Indonesia | **Industrial Technology Development Project**

Project ID: P003978

TM: Lily Uy Hale

Loan amount: US$38.5 million

Development Objective: To enhance the competitiveness of industry, and particularly of small and medium-size enterprises (SMEs) | ▨ Improving MSTQ services, and upgrading and assessing calibration laboratories under the National Calibration System to provide better service to R&D centers
▨ Improving the provision of technology upgrading services to SMEs by creating a Technology Services Matching Grant Scheme (DAPATI)
▨ Improving the productivity of public R&D institutions to provide better services to SMEs
▨ Improving industrial and technology policy formulation | Closed 2001 | The project enabled the government to take a more proactive stance in the focusing of industrial technology development policies and programs such that they align more clearly with private sector development and industrial competitiveness. The use of twinning partners aided local institutions through the transfer of R&D management practices, and led also to the investigation of new avenues of technology and business development and of human resource development (for example, in the training of leaders in R&D management). The business reorientation of the R&D institutions exceeded the original expectations, notably inspiring some institutions to set up spin-off companies. Income of Research and Development Center for Applied Chemistry from industry increased from 24 percent to 84 percent during the project. Overall income of the Agency for the Assessment and Application of Technology increased from 10 billion rupiah (about US$1 million) to 15 billion rupiah (US$15 million) in three years, and RDCAC's self-financing jumped in the last year of the project from 16 percent to 43 percent. The institutional strengthening component of the project completed a study on the formulation of an industrial master plan and policy that led to the creation of the National Competitiveness Council, headed by the Coordinating Minister for Economic Affairs. The government additionally is preparing a green paper that will take note of the discussions and decisions from the workshop and that is intended to serve as the policy guidance for future R&D development. The deeper objective of this workshop was to persuade the Ministry of Finance to revise Law 20 to allow budgetary flexibility of the R&D institutes. Overall, the project served the intended purpose of having |

(continued)

Fiscal Year	Country	Project Information	Project Components	Status	Outcomes
					a demonstration effect, influencing the overall technology policy and expenditure in the direction of commercialization, accountability, and transparency.
1996	China	**Technology Development Project** Project ID: P003600 TL: Lily Uy Hale Loan amount: US$200 million **Development Objective:** To support the government's reforms in technology policy and institutions, and to promote the development and adoption by industry of cleaner, productivity-enhancing technologies	▧ Supporting engineering research centers (ERCs) to assist in restructuring part of China's R&D capability into market-responsive corporations, with the objective of adapting, developing, and diffusing technologies ▧ Supporting complementary investments in technology-based public services, such as the modernization of the National Institute of Metrology and a technical assistance program for a Productivity Center	Closed 2002	All of the 47 ERCs financed under the project were converted to either a limited liability corporation (LLC), a stock limited corporation (SLC), a state-owned enterprise (SOE), or were absorbed as R&D centers of other LLC/SLC/SOEs. The 47 ERCs were mostly in the fields of clean production and environmental protection technology, energy saving technology, and information for industrial production. Starting in 1996, the Project Office and Golden China Corporation organized (with Bank assistance) national ERC workshops almost every year, with an average participation of around 200, as well as a number of study tours. The ERCs additionally organized their own overseas and domestic training in management and transformation, with more than 160 people participating in 36 teams. In 2001 the State Development & Planning Commission organized an ERC exhibit and an ERC Technology and Investment Conference at the Third Shenzen High Technology Fair. The ERC fair, which showcased some 200 achievements, received 150,000 visitors, and 19 ERCs signed contracts worth a total of RMB260 million (US$32 million). The 47 ERCs now employ about 6,900 people, more than 50 percent of whom have senior or intermediate professional titles. They have transferred some 600 major research results, implemented more than 26,500 technology transfer contracts, and established some 60 subsidiaries, including joint ventures. According to infor-

(continued)

mation presented by the GCC, the aggregate gross income of ERC projects was a cumulative RMB7,225 million (US$870 million). Additionally, the National Institute of Metrology and Productivity Center were established to complement the transformation of the ERCs through improved public services. The institute reported progress toward higher primary standards of measurement and in establishing new standards for the calibration of engineering parameters. The Productivity Center established and improved databases and websites for standardization, quality management, service measurement, and experimental conditions. To date, more than 2,000 SMEs have accepted services from the PC.

| 1996 | Mauritius | **Higher and Technical Education Project**
Project ID: P001923
TM: Peter R. Moock
Loan amount: US$16.0 million
Development Objective: To support the government's tertiary education program as outlined in the 1991 Education Sector Master Plan (ESMP), which aimed to produce the human resources required to support a more competitive economy | ■ Strengthening the University of Mauritius (UoM) by: (a) upgrading staff and facilities to improve education quality; (b) increasing the number of qualified graduates; (c) improving links with employers to increase curriculum relevance and graduate marketability; (d) developing viable postgraduate education and research programs in strategic areas; and (e) enhancing the efficiency of UoM operations
■ Rationalizing polytechnic education by: (a) improving the quality of faculty, curricula, and facilities; (b) supporting the development of business programs and strengthening links with UoM and the private sector; and (c) strengthening the policy and analytic capacity of the Management Trust Fund (MTF) | Closed 1999, 1.8 years ahead of schedule. Total loan disbursed was US$3.1 million | The project successfully helped to produce more high-level and mid-level professionals, but the capacity of the higher-level ones to raise the quality and diversity of Mauritius's industry and service sectors is uncertain, given that quality improvements at UoM were marginal. In terms of staff upgrading, it was envisaged that 120 staff would undergo training to increase the percentage of Ph.D.-holders from 25 percent in 1994 to 55 percent by 2006. After a slow start and three years of implementation, eight staff members had obtained doctorates and 17 had obtained master's degrees. The development of the library and the Faculty of Engineering was not achieved, as a result of the need to undertake a space audit and poor communications and collaboration between the Bank, UoM, and the Ministry of Public Infrastructure. Efforts to improve labor market relevance were marginally successful, and efforts to expand research and link it with the strategy of the Mauritius Research Council failed: only four research projects were submitted for financ- |

Fiscal Year	Country	Project Information	Project Components	Status	Outcomes
					ing and none of these went forward because the government would not approve the use of loan funds for consumable materials. The objective of improving quality and relevance was achieved, with almost all staff receiving training in Singapore or Australia. Work aimed at improving management and labor market linkages was partially successful. The industry–faculty advisory committees met regularly and polytechnic students were readily absorbed into the job market: 65 percent of Droopnath Ramphul graduates were employed six months after graduation. Five factors primarily were responsible for the unsatisfactory results of the project: (a) unrealistic staff development targets; (b) low levels of commitment at UoM; (c) lack of familiarity with Bank procedures; (d) poor communication between government agencies; and (e) rigid regulations. At the request of the government, US$12.0 million of the loan was cancelled. The government and the Bank subsequently agreed that it would be more efficient to close the loan early and complete the project at a more realistic pace using the government's own resources.
1996	Russia	**Standards Development Project** Project ID: P008837 TM: Vladimir Drebentsov Loan amount: US$24 million **Development Objective:** To promote non-	▪ Supporting the creation of a Standards Enquiry Point required by the WTO. It would act as an electronic clearing house and depository for Russian and international standards. ▪ Supporting the harmonization of standards in a joint effort by Russian and foreign experts to conduct a case-by-case inspection of existing standards in	Closed 2001, two years after the scheduled closing date	Overall, the project met its objectives: (a) a WTO inquiry point was established and made operational on international and Russian technical barriers to trade (TBT) in goods; (ii) a solid foundation was laid for extending the functions of the TBT inquiry point to serve as an inquiry point for sanitary and phytosanitary standards; (c) work was begun on the harmonization of Russian technical standards for export products with international standards, with approximately 40 percent of Russian standards harmonized with international stan-

traditional exports by facilitating Russia's accession to the World Trade Organization (WTO)

areas most promising for the manufacture of exports

■ Supporting certification and accreditation by enabling participating entities to conform with the norms that have been established in international agencies, by financing the procurement of equipment for testing centers and supporting an exchange program of Russian and foreign experts to promote the mutual exchange of information and recognition, the overseas training of test engineers and certification personnel in counterpart OECD environments, and accreditation procedures

dards by project completion (as compared to 18 percent at launch); and (d) modernization of the selected Russian testing/certification centers was accomplished, facilitating their international accreditation. These successes together contributed to the increasing openness of Russia's trade—in particular by facilitating WTO accession and harmonization of standards—and to the promotion of Russia's nontraditional manufactured exports. The project was less successful in meeting its revised objective of streamlining the Russian system of testing, certification, and accreditation requirements for imports, however, primarily because of the relatively short time period allowed for this revised project and low government commitment to liberalization in this area. After completion of the project in mid-2001, the push for radical changes in this area came from an acceleration toward WTO accession. Amending domestic laws on standards and technical regulations and certification procedures to bring them into conformity with WTO requirements became a priority in the government plan of legal work for WTO accession that was approved in August 2001. The draft law on technical regulations submitted to the cabinet in March 2002 envisages a dramatic reduction, from about 20,000 to 100, in the number of standards containing mandatory requirements. Likewise, a flexible system of conformity compliance will substitute for the current mandatory premarket certification by a third party of the bulk of goods sold on the domestic market. These project objectives may thus be realized at a later stage.

(continued)

Fiscal Year	Country	Project Information	Project Components	Status	Outcomes
1997	Thailand	**Secondary Education Quality Improvement Project** Project ID: P042259 TM: n/a Loan amount: US$194.7 million **Development Objective:** To help raise the quality of secondary education in science, mathematics, and English. Specifically, (a) to raise the quality of in-service teacher training in the three critical subject areas; and (b) to upgrade the quality of primary and secondary schools through provision of modern science and language training equipment and laboratory facilities	▓ Supporting quality improvement through financing an institutional development program, including overseas and in-country training, study tours, and fellowship programs to raise teacher qualifications ▓ Assisting the purchase of equipment, furniture, and teaching materials to upgrade science and language facilities ▓ Supporting the financing of civil works projects that will rehabilitate selected primary and secondary schools (to include the funding of equipment-related O&M, project management, and monitoring and evaluation). The selection of project schools is strongly oriented toward rural areas	In progress	ICR not available
1998	Indonesia	**Information Infrastructure Development Project** Project ID: P042169 TM: Robert Schware	▓ Improving the legal and regulatory framework by preparing IPR-related laws and regulations, carrying out policy studies, and strengthening the skills of government staff ▓ Expanding the S&T network of researchers by providing the	In progress	ICR not available

		Loan amount: US$34.5 million **Development Objective:** To enhance private sector participation in the provision of IT, postal, and tourism services, through the removal of barriers to entry	▪ S&T community with more cost-effective access to R&D through an expansion of IPTEKnet ▪ Expanding communications and information networks, postal services, and tourism	
1998	Brazil	**Science and Technology Reform Support (PADCT III) Project** Project ID: P038947 TM: Alcyone Saliba Loan amount: US$155 million **Development Objective:** To improve the overall performance of the science and technology sector by undertaking activities that promote scientific research and technological innovation in an efficient manner	▪ Supporting technology development by supporting cooperative precompetitive research aimed at fostering partnerships among industries, universities, technological institutes, and government agencies; by supporting a matching grant facility, providing two types of grant programs: publicly led cooperative projects to foster partnerships between the public and private sectors for the financing and execution of R&D, and privately led cooperative projects to foster cooperation between individual firms and public sector R&D entities, with the purpose of producing proprietary R&D outputs; and by assisting technology adoption by SMEs to enhance their capacity to innovate ▪ Supporting S&T research by awarding grants for scientific research and for developing regional S&T capacity	In progress ICR not available

(continued)

Fiscal Year	Country	Project Information	Project Components	Status	Outcomes
			▪ Funding sectoral support activities to provide: (a) support to working groups involved with sectoral reform; (b) support for the improvement of sectoral monitoring and evaluation to enhance the quality, coverage, and accessibility of information about the performance of the S&T sector; (c) support for the administering and enforcement of the IPR regime; (d) support for metrology and standards services; and (e) support for an interim fund to provide for the maintenance of scientific equipment		
1999	Chile	**Higher Education Improvement Project** Project ID: P055481 TM: Lauritz Holm-Nielsen Loan amount: US$145.45 million **Development Objective:** To improve the performance of the higher education system in terms of its coherence and efficiency, quality and relevance, and equity	▪ Providing a policy framework and supporting capacity building through: (a) enhancement of the legal and regulatory framework; (b) policy and institutional capacity building; (c) establishment of a management information system; and (d) promotion of technical training ▪ Providing technical assistance to help establish minimum standards and acceptable, recognized levels in educational services ▪ Supporting institutional financing and student aid studies by: (a) establishing a policy for public funding; (b) increasing accountability and developing an institution-building funding methodology; and (c) establishing a competitive fund to promote quality and relevance	In progress	

| 1999 | Mexico | **Knowledge and Innovation Project**
Project ID: P044531
TM: Daniel Crisafulli

Loan amount: US$300 million

Development Objective: To promote the generation, diffusion, and application of knowledge for innovation in support of economic and social development, with emphasis on the stimulation of linkages and the effective diffusion of knowledge for innovation | ▨ Supporting S&T research by stimulating research in fields with scientific, economic, and/or social importance (with an emphasis on promoting quality in research, consolidating and improving peer review, promoting participatory planning, improving human resources training, and integrating young researchers in the system); and through institutional strengthening of the Project Deputy Directorate of Scientific Management Research of National Science and Technology Council, specifically in the areas of monitoring, evaluation, and strategy
▨ Supporting joint action between universities/public research institutes and the private sector by: (a) restructuring public S&T institutes to increase cost recovery while improving client orientation and the effectiveness of service provision in support of industry; (b) matching grants for joint industry–academia projects; (c) providing technical assistance to institutional universities to create and strengthen university outreach offices
▨ Supporting the productivity and competitiveness of firms, particularly SMEs, through (a) a technology modernization program to assist the upgrading of | In progress |

(continued)

Fiscal Year	Country	Project Information	Project Components	Status	Outcomes
		SMEs via a matching grant scheme administered by a decentralized network of local agents; and (b) private regional/sectoral institutional technology support centers that aim to strengthen and promote the creation of demand-driven services			
2000	Turkey	**Industrial Technology Project** Project ID: P009073 TM: Vinod K. Goel Loan amount: US$155 million **Development Objective:** To assist in the harmonization of the domestic technology infrastructure with European Customs Union (ECU) standards; and to help firms upgrade their technological capabilities to improve the competitiveness of industry, both at home and overseas	▪ Strengthening of IPR services; specifically, by assisting harmonization of Turkey's IPR regime with building, WTO, and ECU standards ▪ Strengthening of metrology services through investments in infrastructure, with the goals of serving a larger section of Turkish industry and gaining the acceptance of European bodies. ▪ Supporting the restructuring of R&D institutions to make them more industry-oriented ▪ Supporting technology upgrades and innovation by small firms by providing matching loans for technology development, promoting goods, and promoting information dissemination to SMEs; and by exploring the possibilities of technology service centers, venture capital, and Technoparks.	In progress. Expected closing is December 2004	The second Industrial Technology Project in Turkey has been very successful and well-received thus far. The project is a follow-up to the first Technology Development Project. It continues to support UME, transforming it into a world-class metrology institution capable of meeting 80–90 percent of Turkish industry's metrology needs today, and the Technology Development Foundation of Turkey, a privately-managed NGO set up as a public-private partnership. The TTGV, in addition to its original technology financing mandate (it has financed about 200 projects), has become a catalyst in supporting VC funds (two VCCs were set up with TTGV's equity participation) and also supports two technoparks (it has added a matching grant scheme to its operations). This project is also setting up two innovation centers and a start-up capital fund. In addition, its competitive Technology Support Services (TSS) grant scheme has benefited about 600 SMEs. The TTGV has developed into a diverse technology financing institution and has changed the entire technology financing culture in Turkey. Most of its projects have resulted in the commercialization of R&D outputs. The Project has also supported the restructuring of the network of Turkish RDIs and the reconfigura-

					tion of MAM (a group of eight leading RDIs), and has improved the IPR regime through the strengthening of the Turkish Patent Institute (TPE). MAM has increased its contractual research base, and was about 49 percent self-sufficient in 2003, targeting 65–70 percent self-sufficiency by 2006. The IPR regime is improving its alignment with ECU and WTO requirements and TPE is developing into an international-level institution.
2000	Chile	**Millennium Science Initiative (MSI)** Project ID: P063386 TM: Lauritz Holm-Nielsen Loan amount: US$5.0 million **Development Objective:** To improve performance in the science and technology sector by supporting the advanced training of Chilean scientists by world-class scientists engaged in cutting-edge research	▪ Supporting management structure (the MSI Directorate) through the establishment and operation of a board of directors, program committees, and an Implementation and Management Unit (IMU) ▪ Supporting monitoring and evaluation studies by financing studies, publications, remuneration of program committees and IMU personnel, and administrative costs ▪ Supporting competitive funding for scientific excellence in projects to carry out scientific research; doctoral and post-doctoral training programs/opportunities; and networking, outreach, and other activities aimed at promoting scientific excellence ▪ Promoting scientific excellence through research visits to establish formal and informal connections to top centers and institutions; programs for the exchange of researchers and post-graduate and graduate students; the design and deliv-	Closed 2002	Science and technology is receiving increased attention by the GoC and other governments in the region. The project has established a fair, open, and merit-based selection process which have been acknowledged and accepted by the scientific research community. The project has improved the productivity of Chile's top researchers. Opportunities for and the quality of advanced training have increased. A several forms of collaboration increased significantly under the project's auspices. A monitoring and evaluation base is being built which can serve as a platform for improved S&T policy. A light and effective administrative structure for science funding was established. This structure includes the Board of Directors, chaired by the Minister of Planning, a Program Committee comprised of internationally-recognized scientists, and an Executive Secretariat staffed by competent and respected personnel. Soon after project effectiveness, the first round of competitive funding was very efficiently completed. Three scientific institutes and five scientific nuclei (selected from amongst 75 applicants) were established and are operating for two years. Over 150 key research workers including some of the best Chilean scientists, are directly funded under the Institutes and Nuclei grants. These include 66 graduate

(continued)

Fiscal Year	Country	Project Information	Project Components	Status	Outcomes
			ery of international advanced courses; and the dissemination of lessons learned. The program also finances the remuneration of researchers, fellowships for doctoral and postdoctoral students, travel expenditures, and publications		students (32 financed fully by the MSI and 34 partially funded) and 25 post-doctoral fellows. During project implementation, 47 PhD. diplomas were granted to the financed graduate students.
2000	China	**Higher Education Reform Project** Project ID: P046051 TM: Hena Mukherjee Loan amount: US$50 million (Loan—US$20 Million and Credit for US$50 Million) **Development Objective:** To improve the quality and relevance of undergraduate basic science and engineering programs through integrated reforms in curriculum and teaching methodology	▓ Improving teaching and learning by enhancing the quality of undergraduate science and engineering programs ▓ Using partnerships and networks to extend reforms to the weaker partner institutions in poor or inaccessible areas ▓ Supporting institutional capacity for change by strengthening institutional planning and administration, central coordination, and management	In progress	
2001	Nicaragua	**Competitiveness Learning and Innovation Loan Project** Project ID: P070016 TM: Michaela Weber	▓ Developing effective and inclusive business clusters, by (a) undertaking initial cluster diagnostic and benchmarking assessments; (b) identifying cross-cluster business environment constraints and reform	In progress	

	Amount: US$5.0 million **Development Objective:** To test private–public partnerships for their ability to develop consensus and introduce reform on business environment issues; and to pilot sustainable IT-based business development services (BDSs)	proposals; (c) improving the productivity, quality, and efficiency of the sectors represented in the clusters; (d) continuing the broad promotion and dissemination of and training in the methodology; and (e) establishing cluster information networks ■ Piloting reforms for competitiveness policies, institutions, and administrative procedures related to private sector development by strengthening the participation of the private sector in policy reform ■ Increasing management capacity to develop a consensus on competitiveness policy with public–private partnerships	
2001	Venezuela **Millennium Science Initiative** Project ID: P066749 TM: Lauritz B. Holm-Nielson Loan amount: US$5 million **Development Objective:** To strengthen R&D capacity so that the country can gain access to global knowledge and improve its knowledge base in areas that are key to its economic and social development; and to demonstrate	■ Supporting capacity building of the new Ministry of Science and Technology through assisting the establishment and operations of the board of directors, the program committee, and the Implementation and Management Unit (IMU); providing technical assistance in selection of the Centers of Excellence (CEs) and Nuclei for Excellent Research (NER); assisting development of a proposal to scale up and institutionalize the project; and assisting M&E studies. Under this component the program will finance studies, publications, the remuneration of the program committee and the IMU's personnel, and administrative costs	In progress

(continued)

Fiscal Year	Country	Project Information	Project Components	Status	Outcomes
		the effectiveness of transparent, merit-based allocation procedures and investigator autonomy in improving the quality and efficiency of scientific research and training	▪ Supporting the competitive fund for scientific excellence by assisting the funding of research projects at the three CEs and 8–12 NERs ▪ Supporting the network for the promotion of scientific excellence		
2002	Indonesia	**Global Distance Learning Network Project** Project ID: P073970 TM: Jerry G. Strudwick Loan amount: US$2.6 million **Development Objective:** To test the potential effectiveness and sustainability of the Global Development Learning Network (GDLN); and to develop appropriate technologies to link the Jakarta-based GDLN center to three regional university centers in the western, central, and eastern regions	▪ Establishing, retrofitting, and equipping the main GDLN center and the three subcenters. The GDLN center will include a video conferencing room with a 30-person capacity for synchronous video interaction (video, data, and voice exchange) between local participants, remote course instructors, and international participants ▪ Supporting the operation of the center and subcenters by (a) financing operation costs on a decreasing basis over the four years of implementation; (b) providing technical assistance for the training of Distance Learning Center staff, periodic evaluation of their O&M effectiveness, and establishment of financial accounts and an annual audit; (c) providing funds for the sponsoring and development of local course content and partnerships; and (d) financing a technology review and upgrade	In progress	

2002	Armenia	**Enterprise Incubator Project** Project ID: P044852 TM: Vladimir G. Kreacic Loan amount: US$5.0 million **Development Objective:** To provide a demonstration effect of company formation in an inhospitable business environment; to provide a demonstration effect of the positive impact of foreign direct investment (FDI) in the IT industry; and to pilot demand-driven mechanisms for the continuous upgrading of IT skills of professionals, third-year students, and work force and enterprise managers and employees	■ Providing telecommunications infrastructure and office space for lease to IT and high-tech companies already operating or financed for start-up ■ Providing business development services to clients, mostly locally owned software companies with typically poor management and marketing skills. A Business Services Center will establish business connections between local IT companies, foreign investors, and clients ■ Providing on-demand technical training for Incubator tenants and for other clients, including university undergraduate and graduate students, at a skills development facility. This component will also provide entrepreneurship grants to IT professionals and students to help them turn their ideas into businesses ■ Supporting IT business surveys to biannually monitor the regulatory environment for the IT cluster firms	In progress
2003	Egypt	**Higher Education Enhancement Project** Project ID: P056236 TM: Mae Chu Chang Loan amount: US$50 million	■ Supporting government efforts to restructure system governance and management such that conditions enable greater sector efficiency and quality. Specific activities to be supported include: (a) reform of legislation governing higher	Under preparation

(continued)

Fiscal Year	Country	Project Information	Project Components	Status	Outcomes
		Development Objective: To create the conditions essential for improving the quality and efficiency of the higher education system; to be achieved through legislative reform, institutional restructuring, and the establishment of independent quality assurance mechanisms and monitoring systems	education; (b) rationalization of funding allocation mechanisms; (c) establishment of a National Quality Assurance Council (NQAC); (d) capacity building and management training; (e) establishment of a higher education enhancement project (HEEPF) ▪ Improving the quality and relevance of university education. The activities supported under this component aim to address quality concerns by responding to the need for new learning technologies and equipment ▪ Supporting efforts to improve the quality and relevance of institutions providing mid-level technical education through assisting consolidation of the middle technical institutes into technical colleges; assisting curriculum design and instructor training; and helping strengthen academic administration and management		
2003	India	**Technical Engineering Education Quality Improvement Project** Project ID: P072123 TM: Shashi K. Shrivastava Loan amount: US$250 million	▪ Supporting competitive funding for institution development. Well-performing engineering institutions, both public and private, would be selected through open competition for assistance in attaining higher standards of education and establishing close linkages with industry, the community, and other institutions. The program would support the following in each institutional	Under preparation	

		Development Objective: To support the development of technical professionals through reforms in the technical/engineering education system, with the goal of raising productivity and competitiveness	development subproject: the promotion of academic excellence, the networking of institutions for quality enhancement and resource sharing, and enhancement of the quality and reach of services to the community and the economy ■ Supporting system management capacity improvement through assisting (a) the development of a modern management style (through the training of policy planners, managers, and administrators from the central and participating state governments); (b) policy and system research studies at the state and national levels; (c) the management of performance, reforms, quality, and efficiency audits; and (d) the establishment of structures and facilities for program management at the central and state levels.
2003	Ukraine	**eDevelopment Project** Project ID: P074885 TM: Andrei Mikhnev Loan amount: US$5 million **Development Objective:** enhance efficiency of the Government's decision-making process for public procurement and documen-	■ The E-Government component provides for development and introduction of the public E-Procurement and E-Documentation flow models aimed at increasing efficiency and transparency of the Government actions. ■ The E-Business Environment component will assess the main bottlenecks in current legislation that hamper e-business growth. Legislative, nonnative and regulatory environment adequate to accelerate enabling on-line transactions will be developed.

(continued)

Fiscal Year	Country	Project Information	Project Components	Status	Outcomes
		tation flow, foster private sector development, and strengthen civil society in Ukraine through the introduction of innovative models of ICT solutions.	▪ The Public–Private E-Dialogue component will provide for on-line tools for an exchange of ideas between public authorities and representatives of private sector and civil society at the national and regional levels. Introduction of these tools would i) improve public sector transparency, and ii) strengthen the role and involvement of civil society in the governance process. The component will strengthen the Ukrainian NGOs and private sector representatives' leadership in public-private partnership.		
2003	Yemen	**Higher Education Learning and Innovation Project** Project ID: P076183 TM: Ousmane Diagana Loan amount: US$5.0 million **Development Objectives:** To assist the government in preparing a higher education reform strategy and to pilot the initial phases of its implementation by helping develop capacity in the newly created Ministry of	▪ Supporting the government in developing (a) a strategy and medium-term development plan for the sector and (b) a legislative and institutional framework promoting improved governance and management ▪ Supporting the process of financial delegation to Yemen's two universities through: (a) the redesign of budget structures and procedures to facilitate flexible allocation of resources and efficient expenditure, and through program budgets with contractual obligations in terms of objectives and performance indicators; (b) the development of an equitable funding mechanism for universities, promoting competition and the achievement of priority objectives, such	Under preparation	

Higher Education and Scientific Research (MHESR)	as the participation of girls and greater diversification of income, through tailored, on-demand courses and services; and (c) the acquisition and adaptation, including related training, of an integrated MIS, permitting the timely tracking of financial transactions and providing other key institutional management information, serving the MHESR and the two universities ■ Improving learning and upgrade opportunities for students and faculty in selected faculties by piloting strategic initiatives with regard to: (a) the evaluation, modernization, and piloting of programs, building on renewal efforts already underway, together with the upgrading of the knowledge and teaching skills of the faculty and support staff; (b) support of program renewal; the design, development, and piloting of an ICT network linking the central libraries and faculty libraries, facilitating faculty and student exchanges via an intranet and providing access to the resources of the Internet; (c) assistance to the two universities in initiating a process of self-evaluation and improvement and the development of agreed standards that could be applied by other public sector universities as a basis for future accreditation; and (d) preparation for the early extension of accreditation to Yemen's private universities

(continued)

Fiscal Year	Country	Project Information	Project Components	Status	Outcomes
2004	Honduras	**Competitiveness Enhancement Project** Project ID: P070038 TM: John Henry Stein, Marialisa Motta Loan amount: US$28 million **Development Objective:** To improve the investment climate and the capacity of local firms to export, to enable the country to take advantage of opportunities under existing and new trade promotion agreements; and to increase the productivity of the private sector, thereby improving overall competitiveness and economic growth, increasing employment, and reducing poverty levels	▪ Improving key elements of the investment climate through efforts to reduce the time taken by and cost of business registration, export, and operation; the reduction of anticompetitive behavior and improvement of consumer protection; and the raising of quality and lowering of infrastructure and logistics costs ▪ Promoting private sector innovation through the creation of Innovation Centers (*Centros de Innovaciones Tecnologicas;* CITEs) to improve productivity; the encouragement of higher-value FDI and of broader linkages between foreign and local firms; and development of a national quality system and education regarding the importance of quality certification, including environmental certification ▪ Improving the skills of the labor force by financing (a) a study of the supply of and demand for training; (b) a review of existing training law and regulations and development of a legal framework to provide incentives to private firms to train their workforce; (c) technical support to reorganization of the National Institute of Professional Training; (d) development of standards and curriculum accreditation to certify private firms that provide training;	Under preparation	

(e) the matching of funds for firms that intend to train their workforce and develop in-service training; and (f) an information campaign to promote awareness of the benefits of training and to strengthen the capacity of enterprises to identify the specific work skills they need

- Enhancing local competitiveness by piloting the creation of local competitiveness strategies in four localities
- Launching a communication campaign on broad themes related to competitiveness
- Strengthening project implementation by supporting the creation of a project implementation unit, financing the employment of specialists and consultants to support it, and funding operational expenses, training, and some equipment

| 2004 | Democratic Republic of Congo | **Private Sector Development and Competitiveness Project**
Project ID: P071144
TM: Ivan Rossignol
Loan amount: US$120 million
Development Objective: To increase the competitiveness of the economy and thereby contribute to economic growth | ■ Improving the investment climate by strengthening the judiciary and improving the legal and fiscal framework, by establishing a private national arbitration center, providing technical and financial support to three commercial tribunals, providing operational support to the judiciary, and disseminating legal information
■ Implementing parastatal reform by strengthening regulatory authority in the telecommunications, transportation, and | Under preparation |

(continued)

Fiscal Year	Country	Project Information	Project Components	Status	Outcomes
			energy sectors through technical assistance and training, and supporting activities to help redundant workers develop new occupations ■ Supporting measures aimed at increasing competitiveness of the economy of Katanga, the leading mining region, by creating new economic opportunities for the workers retrenched from Gecamines and for other parastatals present in Katanga, and by fostering regional economic development		
2004	Chile	**Science for the Knowledge Economy Project** Project ID: P077282 TM: Lauritz Holm-Nielson Loan amount: US$25 million **Development Objective:** To develop an effective innovation system by establishing a strong and coherent policy framework, promoting high-quality S&T activities, and by supporting key interfaces in the innovation system; and to improve the stock of human capital in the	■ Developing a policy framework and an enabling environment for innovation through (a) establishment of an independent advisory board for project management and implementation; (b) development of a coherent strategy, conducive polices, and S&T awareness; and (c) development of a monitoring and evaluation capacity ■ Increasing the capacity of the science base and contributing to social and economic development through three competitive programs that aim to realize excellence in science, advanced human capital, and improvement of the research infrastructure. The project will finance grants, scholarships, and the establishment of a program for major scientific equipment	Under preparation	

		S&T sector, a critical precondition for establishment of a competitive knowledge-based economy	▪ Supporting activities that strengthen linkages between the scientific community, industry, and public sector users of research findings; and building private sector research capacity through the establishment of competitive programs for cooperative research consortia; researchers in industry, and international cooperation in research		
2004	Croatia	**Science and Technology Project** Project ID: P080258 TM: Ekaterina Koryukin Loan amount: US$38 million **Development Objectives:** To reorient the S&T infrastructure (in particular, to strengthen and restructure research and development institutions (RDIs) and promote commercialization of their research outputs); and to upgrade the technological capabilities of enterprises. (Under preparation)	▪ Supporting the restructuring of public RDIs to strengthen their capacity and reorient their research infrastructure to serve the economy through applied research ▪ Supporting the upgrading of the technological capabilities of small firms by helping private enterprises and researchers use, develop, and commercialize new technologies; supporting the strengthening and capacity building of the Business Innovation Center of Croatia (BICRO), the Croatian technology financing institution; and assisting with the specific programs that it will manage, including the granting of financial support to knowledge-based firms and to the Productivity and Quality Facility (a matching small grant scheme for SMEs), to VC funds; and to the setting up and upgrading of technology and R&D centers.	Under preparation	The project is under preparation. The planned board date is fiscal 2004.

(continued)

Fiscal Year	Country	Project Information	Project Components	Status	Outcomes
2004	Turkey	**Knowledge and Innovation Project** Project ID: P083985 TM: Severin Kodderitzsch Loan amount: $100 million (Under preparation)	▦ Support to Enterprise Innovation: This component aims to build on and expand the successful experience accumulated by the previous Industrial technology Projects in Turkey by: (i) scale-up enterprise innovation activities, in particular the identification of potentially innovative SMEs and the provision of technical and financial support at the regional level; (ii) to pilot decentralized approaches in providing innovation support services to SMEs, involving private and public actors (e.g. chambers of commerce and/or industry, universities, NGOs, municipalities, etc); and (iii) to seek ways to increase university and enterprise collaboration through the design of relevant programs. ▦ Information Society Development: integrated in Government's "Turkey e-Transformation Project" this comprises: (1) expanding access to ICT for citizens and enterprises by supporting the operations of a universal access fund and piloting approaches to telecenters; (2) providing e-development capacity building to State Planning Organization (SPO) and other Government agencies in implementing the Government's "e-Transforma-	Under preparation	

tion Project"; and (3) launching e-development pilot applications (e-procurement, on-line registration of citizens and businesses, e-commerce platform, etc).

▓ Developing Skills for the Knowledge Economy: This component would (A) stimulate and finance demand for knowledge economy skills through a grant program to help citizens with an emphasis on young adults just entering the work force and adults already in the workforce with SMEs to access knowledge economy skills training courses; and (B) providing start-up incentives for knowledge economy skill providers by creating incentives for a variety of public and private training suppliers to develop flexible, modular, competency based training content needed to develop new knowledge economy skills training programs and market them to the demand-side financed trainees with an emphasis on SMEs.

BACKGROUND PAPERS AND MATERIALS

Crawford and Brezenoff. 2000. "Review of World Bank Lending for Science and Technology (1980–1999)." Washington, D.C.: World Bank.

Dahlman, Carl. 1999. *The Four Pillars of the Knowledge Economy.* Washington, D.C.: World Bank Institute.

De Ferranti, Perry, Gill, Guasch, Maloney, Sanchez-Paramo, and Schady. 2003. "Closing the Gap in Education and Technology." Washington, D.C.: World Bank.

Draft Project Appraisal Document (2003) for Croatia Science and Technology Project.

Draft Turkey Knowledge Economy Assessment Study report (2003).

Finnish Forest Industries Federation, 2002 (2003). http://english.forestindustries.fi/publications/pocketsize.html

Implementation Completion Report (1989) for Korea Program for Science and Technical Education Project.

Implementation Completion Report (1993) for Mexico Industrial Technology Development Project.

Implementation Completion Report (1993, 1994, 1994) for Korea Technology Advancement Projects (First, Second and Third).

Implementation Completion Report (1995) for Korea Universities Science and Technology research Project.

Implementation Completion Report (1997) for China Rural Industrial Technology (Spark) Project.

Implementation Completion Report (1997) for Korea Science Education and Libraries Computerization Project.

Implementation Completion Report (1998) for India Industrial Technology Development Project.

Implementation Completion Report (1998) for Mexico Science and Technology Infrastructure Project.

Implementation Completion Report (1998) for Turkey Technology Development Project 1.

Implementation Completion Reports (1986, 1989, 1992) for Korea Technology Development Projects (First, Second and Third).

OECD. 2003. *Science, Technology and Industry Scorecard 2003*. Paris.

Project Appraisal Document (1995) for China Technology Development Project.

Project Appraisal Document (1998) for Mexico Knowledge Innovation Project.

Project Appraisal Document (1999) for Chile Millennium Science.

Project Appraisal Document (1999) for Turkey Industrial Technology Project.

Project Appraisal Document (2003) for India Technical Engineering Quality Improvement Project.

Project Concept Notes (2003) for Chile Science for the Knowledge Economy.

Various Back-to-Office and Project Status Reports.

Venezuela Supreme Court Modernization Project website: http://www.tsj.gov.ve/

World Bank. 1999. *World Development Report 1998/99: Knowledge for Development*. Washington, DC. http://www.worldbank.org/wdr/wdr98/ppt.htm

———. 2000. *China's Development Strategy: The Knowledge and Innovation Perspective*. Washington. D.C.

———. 2003. *Lifelong Learning for the Knowledge Economy*. World Bank Group, Education Sector.